T0331639

When Machines Can Be Judge, Jury, and Executioner

Justice in the Age of Artificial Intelligence

Highly Recommended Titles

Artificial Intelligence/Human Intelligence: An Indissoluble Nexus
by Richard J Wallace
ISBN: 978-981-123-287-9
ISBN: 978-981-123-308-1 (pbk)

Intelligent Automation: Welcome to the World of Hyperautomation
Learn How to Harness Artificial Intelligence to Boost Business & Make
Our World More Human
by Pascal Bornet, Ian Barkin and Jochen Wirtz
ISBN: 978-981-123-548-1
ISBN: 978-981-123-559-7 (pbk)

Brain vs Computer: The Challenge of the Century is Now Launched
Second Edition
by Jean-Pierre Fillard
ISBN: 978-981-122-500-0
ISBN: 978-981-122-626-7 (pbk)

What Makes You Clever: The Puzzle of Intelligence
by Derek Partridge
ISBN: 978-981-4513-03-6
ISBN: 978-981-4513-04-3 (pbk)

Impossible Minds: My Neurons, My Consciousness
Revised Edition
by Igor Aleksander
ISBN: 978-1-78326-568-8
ISBN: 978-1-78326-569-5 (pbk)

When Machines Can Be Judge, Jury, and Executioner

Justice in the Age of Artificial Intelligence

Katherine B. Forrest

World Scientific

NEW JERSEY · LONDON · SINGAPORE · BEIJING · SHANGHAI · HONG KONG · TAIPEI · CHENNAI · TOKYO

Published by

World Scientific Publishing Co. Pte. Ltd.

5 Toh Tuck Link, Singapore 596224

USA office: 27 Warren Street, Suite 401-402, Hackensack, NJ 07601

UK office: 57 Shelton Street, Covent Garden, London WC2H 9HE

Library of Congress Cataloging-in-Publication Data
Names: Forrest, Katherine Bolan, 1964–   author.
Title: When machines can be judge, jury, and executioner : justice in the
    age of artificial intelligence / Katherine B. Forrest.
Description: Hackensack, NJ : World Scientific Publishing Co. Pte. Ltd., [2021] |
    Includes bibliographical references.
Identifiers: LCCN 2021009800 | ISBN 9789811232725 (hardcover) |
    ISBN 9789811232732 (ebook other) | ISBN 9789811232749 (ebook other)
Subjects: LCSH: Criminal justice, Administration of--United States--Data processing. |
    Artificial intelligence--Law and legislation--United States. | Judicial process--United States--
    Data processing | Decision making--Moral and ethical aspects--United States.
Classification: LCC KF9223 .F67 2021 | DDC 345.7300285/63--dc23
LC record available at https://lccn.loc.gov/2021009800

British Library Cataloguing-in-Publication Data
A catalogue record for this book is available from the British Library.

For any available supplementary material, please visit
https://www.worldscientific.com/worldscibooks/10.1142/12172#t=suppl

Desk Editor: Amanda Yun

Typeset by Stallion Press
Email: enquiries@stallionpress.com

Printed in Singapore

For Amy, because you solved the formula: Y(8000), +2.

Acknowledgments

I have written many articles before, but this is my first non-fiction book. It was a project that occupied virtually any alleged non-working hours for eighteen months. I spent weekends, nights and early mornings digging, digging, reading and writing. I would not have finished the book without the incredible patience and editorial assistance of my partner, Amy Zimmerman, and my daughter, Jane Baldwin. Both spent countless hours as I headed to the finish line, editing and challenging me. I am so grateful.

I also want to thank Kevin Cain for his thoughtful advice, and Nicolas Economou who has invited me to participate in numerous events where I was able to speak on topics directly relevant to this book.

About the Author

⚖

**K**atherine B Forrest is a former federal judge of the Southern District of New York. She recently returned to private practice at Cravath, Swaine & Moore LLP in New York City, where she focuses primarily on areas of the law involving hi-tech. She is also a regular technology contributor to the *New York Law Journal*, and lectures and publishes frequently on the topic of artificial intelligence.

Contents

⚖

Contents

Introduction

⚖

The same technology that allows Amazon to deliver our packages at warp speeds, Google to personalize our search results, and Facebook to tailor our newsfeeds, is now also used to govern the lives and liberties of millions of people. In today's criminal justice system — whether you're aware of it or not — artifical intelligence (AI) is everywhere: it guides carceral sentences, bail decisions, likehoods of arrest, and even the applications of autonomous military weapons. Put simply, AI is essential to how we, as an American society, dispense justice.

How and why we dispense justice matters. When I was a federal judge, I had to explain the decisions I made about a criminal defendant's liberty. If I denied a bail application, and the defendant had to stay behind bars before trial, I had to explain my reason for that decision. When I sentenced a defendant following a conviction, the law required that I lay out why I chose the type and duration of the imposed sentence. If I sentenced a defendant to home confinement or a halfway house, I had to explain myself. If I sent someone to jail, I had to explain not only the basis of the incarceration, but why I chose a particular length of time. Why 13 months and not 12 or 14? 25 and not 26? The specifics of these particulars matter because the fairness is in the details.

As a public servant, I was accountable not only to myself, the plaintiff and the defendant, but to a larger American ideal: if a judge upholds the law unequally, picking and choosing his definitions of fairness without thought or oversight, then the concept of justice — the bedrock of our Constitutional democracy — disintegrates.

The law guides this thought and oversight; American legal codes reflect theories of justice that provide frameworks for responding to criminal transgressions. In the federal system, where I served as a judge from 2011 to 2018, I specifically depended on a statutory framework and the Sentencing Guidelines when imposing a sentence: these entities reflect a combination of retributive, rehabilitative, and fairness theories of justice. Eventually, I will explain these theories in more depth; for now, however, I will simply highlight what they lack: a purely utilitarian approach.

The utilitarian theory of justice, in which the good for the greatest number of people trumps individual fairness, went out of legal favor hundreds of years ago. It is unacceptable — and, further, unfair — to make generalizations about specific groups for the sake of the greater good. For example, should we incarcerate all young people, since they commit the vast majority of crimes, in order to protect our communities from harm? Of course not. We rightly expect fairness and justice at an individual level.

Yet, even as we claim to prefer a nuanced theory of justice, we have developed, implemented, and given the reins to certain AI tools that act against our best interests. These tools, used in connection with decisions of life and liberty throughout the criminal justice system, tend to prioritize utilitarian concepts that eschew notions of individual fairness in favor of the laws of probability. In short, certain AI tools are currently at odds with the stated principles of the very judicial system that they serve. Moreover, we humans have knowingly established and encouraged this AI-judicial incompatibility. AI tools have not gone rogue; we purposefully designed them this way. Over the past few years, we have made our beds with regards to AI and the criminal justice system — but, as we approach the moment of reckoning, we can choose not to lie in them.

This is a book about how AI tools used in life and liberty decisions embed theories of justice, why the theory of the design and evaluation of these tools matters, and what we should be doing to ensure the most fair and equitable AI-involved outcomes. Ultimately, while I do not believe that we should — or could, even if we wanted to — abandon the use of AI tools in our legal system, I maintain that they cannot continue to exist in their current utilitarian forms if we want the American ideal of justice to survive. I make my argument through two examples of AI that are used in connection with life and liberty decision-making: tools used by criminal justice systems to predict risk and need assessments for offenders (RNAs),[1] and lethal autonomous weapons (LAWs).

Personnel throughout the criminal justice system use AI-enabled RNA tools to assist in predicting a particular defendant's future behavior. These tools are designed to answer questions such as whether a *particular* person is likely to commit crimes or acts of aggression, and, accordingly, to determine the defendant's pre-trial bail or remand, the likelihood that the defendant is violent, or the duration of a convicted defendant's period of incarceration. In other words, the tools have a life-altering impact.

The RNA tools are based in a utilitarian framework: they determine what constitutes the greater community good, based on a specific historical data set, and then apply this general view to render justice to a specific person. And whenever you move from the general to the specific, there is necessarily error — about a 30% rate of error, in the case of RNA tools. Nevertheless, they are still used in clear conscience across criminal justice systems nationwide.

The gravity of this error rate is seriously compounded by embedded biases. I use racial bias as a particularly pernicious example of this throughout the book. That is, if you are non-white, the tool's utility perspective leads to less fair outcomes than if you are white. There are explanations for why this occurs — some of which are intuitive, and most of which we will explore later in the book — but there is little doubt that it does occur.

The bottom line: the utilitarian design and outcomes of RNA tools render them currently ill-suited to the criminal justice context. Justice should be fair according to established principles, not just statistically "safe." So, then, why do we still use tools that are so obviously flawed, that are both inaccurate and unfair? The answer is a problem in and of itself: these tools are useful, cheap, and easy.

Two additional issues exacerbate the consequences of using AI tools: a lack of both transparency and legal accountability. As I will discuss, private companies design and license AI tools to third parties or for a particular governmental

---

1   I use "RNA" and "AI Risk Assessment Tool" interchangeably throughout.

entity. In both cases, there are serious limitations with regard to what is known about how the tools are designed, and therefore how they work and the ways in which they may be biased. Furthermore, the lack of a legal framework requiring disclosure means that individuals whose lives and liberties have been impacted by these tools have limited ability to challenge them. Past challenges have been ad hoc and dealt with inconsistently by the courts. Ultimately, the designers of these AI tools are not held accountable for their serious infringements on human liberty.

Still, the answer is not to stop using predictive risk assessment tools altogether, but to accept that top-down micro-fixes won't work; RNA tools need a bottom-up redesign. Any redesign must prioritize a theory of justice as fairness throughout the tool. An AI tool designed along these lines — which is to say, an AI tool without a utilitarian predisposition — could have a positive, course-altering impact on criminal justice reform nationwide. In a nutshell, the benefit of such a redesign is undeniable: accurate and fair risk assessment tools can reduce implicit and explicit human biases that have contributed to justice not equitably distributed, including, for example, in the unacceptable rate of the incarceration of Black men. Criminal justice reform can be furthered in concrete and lasting ways, but only if the tools are fair.

While most of the book is concerned with the use of RNAs, as a matter of comparison I will also address in brief a second example of AI designed with a utilitarian framework: lethal autonomous weapons. The types of LAWs vary in size and scope: there are airborne drones the size of hummingbirds that can conduct surveillance, pack explosives, and swarm into a group of people, and there are massive sea drones with the ability to surveil, locate, and target larger entities. In both instances, as is the case with most LAWs, these drones operate with humans "outside the loop." That is, the drones operate fully autonomously, acting in the same directed-yet-independent manner as foot soldiers on a battlefield. The power — and danger — of LAWs is in their ability to bypass humans in the direct decision of who, when, and how to kill.

Today, we have gotten used to the idea that drone killing occurs. Military personnel in the United States can target and kill people in far-away places like Pakistan and Yemen in the blink of an eye. These types of drones, the ones that we probably think about when we hear the word "drones," are automated weapons, where a human is always in control — "in the loop" — and the traditional military command structure is in place.

LAWs, however, with their "out of the loop" bypass, take intentional killings a step further. Their autonomous functionality has spurred a hot debate about whether we are entering an era of "killer robots" in which human agency is removed from human killing. The dialogue around LAWs raises practical and moral issues regarding how and whether AI tools can distinguish targets, act proportionately in response to changing contexts, and comply with international humanitarian laws that recognize protection of civilians, humane treatment, and human dignity. As with RNAs, the use of LAWs begs the question of accountability: who is held to task for killings gone wrong or thought to be unethical in some way?

While the details of LAWs's designs are generally military secrets, their uses are not. From what the Department of Defense (DoD) and various branches of the US Government have said and written about them, LAWs are designed according to the essential principles of utilitarianism: to neutralize a person, object, or location for the greater communal good. We also know that LAWs are *not* designed to assess whether deployment in connection with a particular targeted person, object, or location is "fair."

Unlike AI RNA tools, which operate outside of a developed body of law, there is already a large body of international humanitarian law that establishes principles against which the fairness of LAWs should be measured. Moreover, there is an active debate about whether, given their innate characteristics, LAWs could ever meet an adequate standard of fairness. The specifics of this "fairness" standard, including what it looks like and the circumstances of its adjudication, are not yet resolved, leaving an ambiguity that only complicates the hot-button topic of LAWs.

The two halves of the LAWs debate fall on opposite sides of the questions of justice that I pose throughout this book. It is clear that AI tools have the ultimate utilitarian potential. LAWs can keep soldiers out of harm's way while operating more precisely and quickly than any human can. And given that other countries and non-state actors have access to these tools, it seems only fair that we fight back in kind. On the other side of the debate is a fundamental moral quandary: is it fair or ethical to have machines kill humans? And who in this humanitarian minefield, where humans have been removed from the military loop, determines these ethics?

I want to make it clear that I do not propose banning LAWs. At this point in our military history, I believe that would be impossible, and I also believe that LAWs, properly applied, have life-saving potential. Instead, I am going to advocate for a reorientation of LAWs toward the appreciation of grey areas that can directly enhance fairness. LAWs must be taught to recognize when a target's behavior might indicate surrender, retreat, or reduced threat, and when a balance of risk and harm tips in favor of holding fire.

At their most basic level, LAWs are machines that can be taught to follow instructions, and they can be reasonably instructed to respect human life and to be fair. Here, I want to emphasize a central thread of the LAWs conversation that underscores my broader arguments around AI and justice: humans have birthed AI technologies that threaten aspects of our autonomy — including our lives, liberties, and dignities — unless we move swiftly to retake control of our justice systems, and, by extension, our futures.

Before I dive into the core of this argument, I want to outline my experience with issues of AI and justice — how did I, an advocate for conscientious urgency in AI reform, get to this point?

In 2011, I was nominated to serve as a US District Judge for the Southern District of New York. This was a position that I held proudly for over 7 years. During my time on the bench, I imposed over 500 criminal sentences, with each of these sentences incorporating my personal view of a "just" result. This is not to say that I made decisions arbitrarily, or that I sentenced defendants carelessly or without reference to precedential case law. In fact, every single decision I made as a judge, no matter how small, was tied to an acute — and often painful — awareness that I was reshaping someone's future. I thus treated every single decision with the care that this kind of calculation deserves. What I mean by my "personal view of a just result" is that any judge's sentence is a necessarily personal, individual decision — there is no single framework of "justice" that all judges have or use.

Many judges think little about the categorical "theory" of justice that underlies their decisions. Instead, they make determinations based on legal precedent, the arguments from counsel, and their own experiences and judgement. Informed individuality is built into the legal system: from evidentiary rulings to case dismissals to sentencings, everything that comes across a judge's desk is interpreted on case-by-case basis. There is no universal "theory" of federal decision-making.

When it comes to sentencing decisions — some of the most critically life-altering decisions I made — the Sentencing Guidelines provide a roadmap designed to bring a measure of consistency to sentences that federal judges impose across the nation. During a one-week bootcamp, every new federal judge learns how to navigate the Guidelines: how to calculate criminal history points, how to add up points based on the type and quantity of drugs possessed or sold, how to determine points for a criminal transaction that involved the use, brandishing, or discharge of a weapon, and how the points change if anyone was injured. In the back of the physical Sentencing Guidelines book there is a handy grid that helps add up all of these points and translates them into a criminal sentence. There is also a range of Supreme Court precedent that reinforces the validity of the sentences that the Guidelines grid spits out.

I want to emphasize that what the Guidelines say is never final; judges are not Guideline robots. But staying close to the Guidelines helps insulate a sentence against reversal in the higher courts, and district judges are certainly encouraged to insulate themselves against reversal.

The main difficulty with the Guidelines is that they do not understand or contemplate individual circumstances. For example, when the Guidelines suggest a particularly high mandatory minimum for a young man who deals heroin to make ends meet, they fail to take into account his unstable upbringing, rife with emotional abuse and addiction, and his once-promising athletic career that ended after he started failing classes in high school. The Guidelines are not human; we should not expect them to rationally process information like a human does.

A common perception of AI is that it makes decisions based on facts, and that these facts correspond with some representation of the truth. But, like human decision-making, this process of AI decision-making is more complicated than it seems. Human decision-makers (judges, for example) are provided with sets of rules (like the Sentencing Guidelines) that they can use in their decision-making process. However, human decision-makers also implicitly and explicitly draw upon moral and ethical precepts in order to interpret these sets of rules according to their personal sense of right and wrong. In other words, humans often make decisions instinctively.

On the other hand, AI decision-making machines have to be taught everything that they know. Yes, these machines can "learn," but there is always a set of initial rules that is encoded into an AI machine's operating software. Human software developers, as the encoders, therefore directly and indirectly teach AI machines everything they want the AI to know and use.

The issue with this process of encoding is that there is no universal standard of human morality. If all AI machines operate according to some pre-determined version of ethics and morality, we then need to ask: whose version? And why?

Absent from the federal judge bootcamp was a discussion of a judge's theory of justice — I was never instructed to follow some umbrella of deontological or virtue ethics. Absent even from the selection, vetting, or confirmation processes were questions about what theory I might use to guide my decisions, or how I might render a "just" sentence for a person with a particular set of characteristics who had committed a particular crime. In the nomination process, my intellectual qualifications were reviewed, and my personal character was scoured, but my basic conception of justice was never tested. But even if we wanted to test a conception of justice, in what way could we objectively do so?

Meanwhile, we trust AI to make determinations about our lives and liberties, and to make those determinations based on a decidedly utilitarian framework. Any given judge might agree or disagree with such a framework (I would argue few would subscribe wholeheartedly). But nevertheless, that same judge, regardless of his theoretical persuasion, might use AI technology to remand a defendant and determine the defendant's likelihood of recidivism. This reality is problematic, to say the least. Further complicating the problem is that fact that AI may proceed based upon design choices or data that embed structural inequalities, as well as implicit and explicit biases.

This book proceeds in the following way. In Chapter 1, I present the dueling theories of utilitarianism and the Rawlsian theory of justice as fairness. My basic argument is that the legal system in the United States is premised upon a concept of natural rights that is reflected in the Constitution. Every person has a right to personal procedural protections with regard to his liberty interest in the Due Process Clause and equal protection. Utilitarian frameworks that prioritize the majority over those individual rights, such as those found in AI tools, are inconsistent with this understanding of fairness.

In Chapter 2, in order to demonstrate how AI tools follow a utilitarian path, I lay out how they work. I do this briefly and at a high level, providing just enough detail to allow the reader to understand how design choices within the AI tool and the applied data set can all embed forms of human choice. In addition, I discuss how one form of AI design used in some risk assessment tools today, machine learning, can create a black box in which the tool's algorithm is not only opaque to those who use it and are impacted by it, but to its original creators as well. I pick up on this theme in Chapter 3 and discuss some of the transparency issues with regard to AI tools that are being brought to courts today.

In Chapters 4 and 5, I lay out how and why humans and AI tools make discretionary decisions that involve judgment and, in so doing, embed ethical frameworks.

In Chapter 6, I introduce risk assessment generally: it is neither novel nor inherently nefarious. This leads into Chapter 7's discussion of the predictive accuracy of AI risk assessment tools. Accuracy for AI assessment tools is determined through something called a "validation" study. Validation studies for all AI assessment tools demonstrate their essentially utilitarian nature. These studies show high levels of inaccuracy (very often in excess of 30%, and never less than 25%), yet the tools are accepted as "good enough." These studies support my argument that "good enough" for a majority of predictions is not "good enough" for an individual person whose liberty interests are at stake.

In Chapters 8 and 9, I take a deep dive into several AI risk assessment tools. I address a handful of tools used in the state system, with a particular focus on the Correctional Offender Management Profiling for Alternative Sanctions (COMPAS), as well as the federal tool, Post-Conviction Risk Assessment (PCRA). I describe how these tools are based on theories that may be controversial, and how they engage in forms of profiling based on aggregate data derived from unrelated people, in order to inform judges, probation officers, and prosecutors about "who" the offender "is." I also discuss the idea that predictive accuracy is inconsistent with individualized fairness due to the current limitations of the models, a notion that tool designers are increasingly aware of.

Chapter 10 discusses this trade-off between accuracy and fairness. I walk through the evolution of this central debate: it started with questioning whether AI assessment tools were inherently biased against Blacks, followed by a vociferous rejection of that position, and culminated in a compromise of sorts. Tool designers now routinely state that while the tools more frequently predict recidivism for Black offenders, and are more often wrong for Black offenders, this is not a reflection of model inaccuracy. Rather, as they point out, the models are correctly applying historical data sets with disproportionately high arrest rates for Black people. The clear issue with this angle, which designers must acknowledge more plainly moving forward, is that the models are applying outdated — or, "historical" — understandings of criminality to an updated set of legal codes and theories of liberty.

The final chapter provides a foil to the set of risk assessment tools: LAWs. Unlike domestic decisions about liberty, which are supposed to be based on fairness and natural rights, military weapons have typically been utilitarian by design. LAWs, however, have the potential to bring military weapons deployments more in line with the Rawlsian idea of justice as fairness. With the increased accuracy and decision-making speed that LAWs afford, there is the potential to clarify a standard of moral fairness in the field of autonomous weaponry — a standard that the designers of state and federal risk assessment tools must similarly strive to meet.

Overall, AI capabilities provide opportunities for humans to increase fairness and access to liberty. But there are limitations in certain tools, such as those in the risk assessment area. We must recognize those limitations, name them for what they are, and make regulatory and design decisions accordingly.

Chapter 1
Utilitarianism versus Justice as Fairness

⚖️

The AI assessment tools that we employ throughout the criminal justice system use a utilitarian framework of justice to make decisions on life and liberty. The utilitarian framework necessarily privileges the majority over the minority. In other words, these AI tools sacrifice fairness at the individual level. If a defendant is Black, or poor, or a member of whichever population that the algorithm has singled out as especially criminal, then the algorithm — which systematically interprets harsh treatment of this defendant as beneficial for the population at-large — may suggest that the defendant presents a particularly high risk of recidivism, resulting in remand before trial, or a longer period of incarceration at sentencing. Is this an efficient way of delivering "justice"? Definitely. But is it a fair way of delivering "justice," in line with our American tradition of individual rights and liberties? Absolutely not.

In this chapter, I am going to contrast the utilitarian principles that AI tools currently employ with a framework that, I argue, better prioritizes the foundational ideals of our criminal justice system: John Rawls's concept of "justice as fairness." An analysis of American legal theory and the criminal justice system reveals that justice as fairness is the historical status quo: the Rawlsian articulation of justice, which expects that certain natural rights will be protected at an individual level, is foreshadowed in the Constitution. It is not a stretch, then, to say that justice as fairness is literally embedded in our conception of American society. If we as a country have defined ourselves according to one theory of justice, then our AI tools can and should follow suit. Alternatively, a worst-case AI scenario could allow utilitarian principles to undermine — and therein override — the pillars of individual liberty that uphold our constitutional legal system; these terms are extreme, but they illustrate the potential perils ahead.

Jeremy Bentham first popularized utilitarianism as a moral and political philosophy in late 18th century England. Concerned about the tyrannical rule of minority interests throughout the French Revolution, Bentham idealized the concept of a majoritarian society. The government, Bentham wrote, should focus on making as many of its constituents as happy as possible, even if that means ignoring some conflicting minority interests. This disregard for minority interests is not a wholly callous calculation: in Bentham's view, the deliberate overlook of the minority is a necessary evil of the majority's greater welfare:

> A measure of government (which is but a particular kind of action, performed by a particular person or persons) may be said to be conformable to or dictated by the principle of utility, when in like manner the tendency it has to augment the happiness of the community is greater than any which it has to diminish it.[1]

The issue with entertaining minority interests, Bentham argues, is that the result will never be worth the effort. A minority faction, by definition, can never account for the greatest amount of happiness among the governed; only a properly governed majority faction can reach that standard. Why, then, should a government concern itself with interests which are most likely to detract from community welfare?

The utilitarian framework is a "consequentialist" one. This essentially means that the utilitarian lawmaker formulates policy according to its ultimate consequences, with little thought to potentially negative side effects. In other words, for the utilitarian, the ends always justify the means. The classic "trolley problem" helps to illustrate this ends-focused approach: if there are five people tied to one set of trolley tracks and one person tied to a second set of trolley tracks, then the purely ends-focused utilitarian will always send the trolley

---

1 J. Bentham, *The Principles and Morals of Legislation* (Amherst, NY: Prometheus Books, 1988), p. 3. Rt.

down the track with just one person, viewing the tragedy of the one lost life as a consequence of the survival and happiness of the five folks who were spared. Setting aside the quasi-murderous force of this example, it is easy to see that one can approach this thought experiment as a decision-making framework that favors majority interests at the expense of the individual.

The "trolley problem" also brings up a main flaw of early utilitarianism: It is relatively brutal — and arguably morally inhuman — to sacrifice the entire concept of individual welfare. The American legal scholar H.L.A. Hart points to this flaw in an apt critique of "pure" utilitarianism:

> [There is an] unbridgeable gap between pure utilitarianism, for which the maximization of total aggregate general welfare or happiness is the ultimate criterion of value, and a philosophy of basic human rights, which insist on the priority of principles protecting, in the case of each man, certain aspects of individual welfare and recognizing these as constraints on the maximizing aggregative principle of utilitarianism.[2]

Many scholars, including John Stuart Mill, agree with Hart. In any decision-making context, there is a "philosophy of basic human rights" that sets constraints on utilitarian applications; in real life, the "trolley problem" does not occur in a moral vacuum. Mill, also writing in the 19th century, expanded on Bentham's views. For Mill, there is a specific utility in the recognition of certain individual rights within the context of serving the majority:

> [The meaning of Utility] is a mere form of words without rational signification, unless one person's happiness, supposed equal (with the proper allowance made for kind), is counted for exactly as much as another's . . . The equal claim of everybody to happiness in the estimation of the moralist and the legislator, involves an equal claim to all the means of happiness, except in so far as the inevitable conditions of human life, and the general interest, in which that of every individual is included, set limits to the maxim; and those limits ought to be strictly construed.[3]

---

2 H. L. A. Hart, *Essays in Jurisprudence and Philosophy* (Oxford: Oxford University Press, 2001), p. 188.

3 J. S. Mill, "On the Connection between Justice and Utility", *Utilitarianism*, Chapter 5.

The decisive point of this fragment is the idea of an "equal claim." The conditions of a happy society presuppose the equal value of happiness among all individuals; that is, everyone has an equal right to happiness, and every individual's happiness is equally valid. Thus, if a government claims to be utilitarian, then it must acknowledge the individual's equal claim on happiness — the individual's right to attain as much happiness as every other individual — in order to assess and govern the general welfare. In other words, any properly-utilitarian government has a necessary interest in the protection, at a very basic level, of an individual right.

In the context of justice theory, here Mill begins to bridge the gap between Bentham and the American ideal of justice — an ideal which I believe aligns with John Rawls's view of justice as fairness. Bentham argues for pure utilitarianism: a government must be totally dictated by majority interests. Mill argues for a basic understanding of individual rights: a government must protect the individual in order to preserve the majority. These political philosophies struck a chord in post-French-Revolution Europe. But a nascent United States government was not so persuaded.

Emerging from years of colonial rule in which individual rights were categorically subjugated, Americans were eager to overhaul the entire idea of government. The following passage by Hart places the contrast between utilitarianism and the vision of the Founding Fathers into historical perspective:

> The crucial difference between [utilitarianism and natural rights] thus opposed in 1776 is that utilitarianism is a *maximizing* and collective principle requiring governments to maximize the total net sum or balance of the happiness of all its subjects, whereas natural right is *distributive* and individualizing principle according priority to specific basic interests of each individual subject.[4]

Even as Bentham and the authors of the Declaration of Independence worked contemporaneously, they envisioned opposite priorities for their respective governments. In Bentham's utilitarian framework, governments "maximize the

---

4 *Essays* 8, p. 182.

total net sum or balance the happiness of all it subjects," whereas the Founding Fathers incorporated the "individualizing" principles of natural rights into the nation's founding documents. No other document in American history better highlights this civic faith in natural rights than the Declaration of Independence itself:

> We hold these truths to be self-evident, that all men are created equal, that they are endowed by their Creator with certain unalienable Rights, that among these are Life, Liberty and the pursuit of Happiness. That to secure these rights, Governments are instituted among men, deriving their just powers from the consent of the governed. That whenever any Form of Government becomes destructive to these ends, it is the Right of the People to alter or to abolish it, and to institute new Government, laying its foundation on such principles and organizing its powers in such form, as to them shall seem most likely to effect their Safety and Happiness.[5]

No one can accuse the Founding Fathers of sublimating the happiness and welfare of the majority — indeed, the colony sought independence from the "destructive" monarchy in the first place in order to "effect [America's] Safety and Happiness." From a distance, that rationale feels relatively utilitarian. Yet, it is the mechanism of this new government — its total devotion to the maintenance of "certain unalienable rights" among the governed — that differentiates its founding philosophy from both Bentham and Mills. At its core, America is a nation of individual rights: the right to life, the right to liberty, and the right to pursue happiness.

This guardianship of the individual carries into the United States' foremost legal doctrine, the Constitution. When the framers of the Constitution added the Bill of Rights, they did more than sweeten the conditions of the document's ratification: they executed an eternal guarantee to the protection of the rights of the American individual. The amended Constitution ensures to every person the right to speak, associate, and practice religion freely; to the due process of law in instances concerning the revocation of life, liberty, or property; to a trial by jury; to the freedom from cruel and unusual punishment; to the confrontation

---

5 Declaration of Independence.

of witnesses who are alleging a crime; and to the equal protection of the laws. Even with just a surface-level analysis of the document, it is impossible to argue against the Constitution's safeguard of individual freedoms.

Clearly, then, utilitarian philosophy should not dictate the American criminal justice system. It makes little sense that a majority-focused doctrine would rule over a society predicated on natural — that is, individual — rights. John Rawls reiterates this sentiment in *A Theory of Justice* (1971) with a "modern critique" of pure utilitarianism:

> The thrust of the modern critique consists of a claim that utilitarianism "does not take seriously the distinction between persons," since it licenses the imposition of sacrifices in individual cases whenever this can be shown to advance aggregate welfare. Persons on this view are of no intrinsic value, but are merely receptacles for the experiences which will increase or diminish the sole intrinsic value, namely aggregate welfare.[6]

Rawls's criticism rightly identifies the lack of "intrinsic value" that utilitarianism assigns to the individual. Expanding on his point — that the utilitarian is concerned only with the individual case as a microcosm of the aggregate welfare — brings us to the conclusion that natural rights philosophy, and therefore the Constitution and the entire American legal system, are incompatible with fundamentally utilitarian thought.

Instead, Rawls proposes a theory of "justice as fairness," which privileges the liberty and equality of the individual over the aggregate:

> My aim is to present a conception of justice which generalizes and carries to a higher level of abstraction the familiar theory of social contract . . . the guiding principles of justice for the basic structure of society are the object of the original agreement. They are the principles that free and rational persons concerned to further their own interests would accept in an initial position of equality as defining the essential terms of their association. These principles are to regulate all further agreements: they specify the kinds of

---

6 *Essays*, p. 194, citing J. Rawls, *A Theory of Justice*, Rev. edn. (Cambridge, MA: Harvard University Press, 1971), p. 187.

social cooperation that can be entered into and the forms of government that can be established.[7]

In short, Rawls views a just society as a society in which every individual creates and abides by laws as if they were in "an initial position of equality." His proposed "initial position" is equivalent to a blank social slate: if you were creating a hypothetical society, where no one in the society — not even you — knew how much fiscal or social capital they had before entrance into the society, what laws would you write? How would you govern if you knew you might be on the receiving end of inequality? You would probably govern far more fairly than if you knew that you already had a leg up on everyone else. Rawls argues that rational individuals are naturally inclined — under conditions where all else is equal — to allow all persons equal access to a full set of basic liberties. This idea of blind governance, with its emphasis on protection of individual rights above all else, is why I believe justice as fairness is the appropriate framework for AI tools in the American legal system.

Both the utilitarian and justice as fairness frameworks posit that how societies dispense justice matters. Needless to say, when laws are administered arbitrarily or for the benefit of a few, civil unrest and revolutions can follow. But similarly, when the majority receives privileges denied to a minority, there are calls for reform. The 1964 Civil Rights Act and the 1965 Voting Rights Act were specifically crafted to enfranchise a vulnerable racial minority. The Supreme Court has repeatedly ruled that the Fourteenth Amendment's Equal Protection Clause means that laws must apply to all populations equally, regardless, for example, of race and gender. We protect — or at least attempt to protect — minorities in other areas of the legal system, so why not do the same with AI?

Our criminal justice system allows the use of AI tools that are only sometimes accurate for utilitarian reasons: the tools add the perception of a known and objective analysis to what is otherwise an unknown human decision-making process. While we hope that human judges can always make the correct decision with the information presented to them, we have no guarantee that they can

---

7 *Ibid.*, p. 10.

do so. Judges are almost always informed, but, unfortunately, they are not always right. Meanwhile, AI risk assessment tools are fed hard, observable data, and are designed to produce results according to an algorithm. Based on this perception of mathematical rigor and data-based decisions, various actors in the criminal justice system decided that AI could take uncertainty out of aspects of the judicial system; the decision was made to consider individual cases en masse — to go the utilitarian route.

While this ostensibly methodical deliverance of justice may seem like a good idea, we have already seen that the tools only get it right around 70% of the time. In no other area of the criminal justice system do we accept a known error rate of approximately 30%. Instead, our understanding is that a fair dispensation of justice requires that with regard to each and every person, and each and every liberty decision, we attempt to get it right 100% of the time. When we see where the 30% rate of inaccuracy comes from, there is even greater cause for concern. Risk assessment tools make decisions based on third party data sets: the recorded behavior of a majority of people in a data set present a pattern, and that pattern is generalized to a set of characteristics in order to predict behavior at an individual level. That is, the patterns found in the data of accumulated arrest, conviction, and probation violation records provide the basis for predictions at an individual level as to how likely a person is to comply with bail terms, recidivate, or commit a violent act. When the data comes from the Stop and Frisk era, or from the ongoing War on Drugs, or any instance of over-policing in low-income communities, then the writing is on the wall for defendants outside of the 'majority'.

The US Constitution requires fairness at an individual level. It requires that all individuals enjoy equal protection under the laws. It does not allow AI tools a "technical exclusion" to the equal protection doctrine because they are as yet unable to achieve true fairness. Instead, constitutional principles require that when tools are known to result in unfairness they not be used. Human decision-making may be imprecise, but at least it meets the standard of justice — or something like it — at an individual level. When humans fall short, at least we can hold them personally accountable.

From any perspective, the crux of the AI issue is unavoidable: employing a utilitarian framework in the context of liberty decisions is not only a departure from the tradition and expectation of individual fairness ingrained in the United States Constitution and the American criminal justice system, but can also lead to a dangerous perpetuation of structural inequalities.

Chapter 2
AI and How It Works

⚖

J ust a few years ago, there were hundreds of artificial intelligence (AI) tools. Now there are thousands upon thousands. These days, we can use AI to unlock our phones with our faces, put a Tesla on autopilot, ask Siri to call our mothers, or listen to a personalized playlist on Spotify. So much of our daily life is affected by AI that we often do not even realize we are using it.

Yet, while AI is a broad field that encompasses a variety of non-human rational decision-making and learning capabilities, most of what we actually use is called "narrow" AI — that is, AI which is oriented towards the completion of a specific task. An example of narrow AI would be a Roomba that is set to clean the living room floor, or a Google Home that we ask to reorder our cat litter.[1] AI-enabled RNA tools and LAWs are used for far graver tasks, but are in fact also task-oriented narrow AI.

At the outset of this discussion, I want to note that I will only be commenting on one form of narrow AI: tools designed to make behavioral predictions. My goal here is quite modest. On a basic level, I am going to outline the design and function of AI tools used for predictive decision-making in the criminal justice area. Within the context of that type of AI tool, I will highlight how theories of justice can be embedded in design features, as well as how the biases reflected in AI design and data sets permit the use of these tools to perpetuate and create unfairness and disparate impact.

---

1 General AI is the opposite: it is AI able to think and problem solve broadly as a human does. There is a debate among scientists as to whether General AI is actually achievable and if so, when.

Recent innovations allowing increased computing power and the availability of large data sets ("big data") have led to an explosion of AI used risk assessment tools. That computing power allows the complex algorithms that underly narrow AI to process vast quantities of data upon which the AI relies for its "knowledge." In short, computing power allows AI to learn, and data gives it something to learn.

It is impossible to overstate the importance of AI's ability to learn. For decades, computers did what we told them to do, in the way that we told them to do it. There is a predictability with intelligence-limited software: we can understand exactly how it does what it does, because we designed it that way.

AI is different. Like all software, it is a human creation — we are its "human progenitors." But unlike its intelligence-limited cousins, AI is not constrained to what its humans tell it to do, or how to do it. Rather, AI has the ability *to learn*, and, from what it learns, to make predictions based upon its independent assessment of probabilities drawn from the data.

A simple way to distinguish sophisticated software that does no more than carry out instructions from AI enabled software tools is by understanding the difference between software *with learning* and software that *can learn*. In other words, non-AI software already knows everything that it needs to know in order to function. AI software, meanwhile, knows everything that it needs and then some: unlike non-AI software, AI software can build on its basic platform of knowledge over time, learning things that it was never taught by humans. Put simply, AI software is smart.

AI's Building Blocks

Algorithms are the building blocks of many AI-enabled software tools, including the ones that I will focus on.[2] An algorithm is essentially the "brain" of the AI tool: it provides a set of rules and instructions as to how information or data should be analyzed and utilized. There are three aspects of algorithms to which

---

2   A terrifically readable book that discusses the different types of algorithms used in AI is P. Domingos' *The Master Algorithm* (Basic Books, 2015). This book is as clear an articulation as I have found of the many differences between the various algorithms used with AI, including such exotic-sounding creatures as recursive algorithms, dynamic programming algorithms, backtracking algorithms, or a brute force algorithm. For my purposes, I'm only going to explain the basic concepts of inputs, weightings, and data sets, but I highly recommend Domingos's work to understand the more complex interactions.

I want to pay particular attention, because we will be returning to them again and again as we explore the issues with risk assessment software: *inputs*, *weightings* of those inputs, and *data sets*.

The algorithm is designed to identify statistical patterns in data about events that have already occurred or are occurring, and, from those patterns, it predicts how future events with similar characteristics are likely to unfold. Still, algorithms that predict the future aren't crystal balls; they don't always guess accurately. The ambiguity in this prediction process comes from the fact that algorithms' predictions are based on probabilities, which always leaves room for error when compared to actual events. This is the very beginning of understanding how the 30% failure rate in AI assessment tools can occur.

To an extent, an algorithm functions like a cooking recipe. The inputs of the algorithm are like ingredients — flour, sugar, water. The weightings of the inputs are like recipe measurements — 1 cup versus 2 cups. The data set would be all versions of the recipe contained in an identified group of cookbooks. But, because AI tools are able to learn beyond their initial instructions and come up with predictive answers, this cooking analogy eventually falls short. An AI algorithm would do more than scan all versions of a recipe, identify patterns, and then execute a version that it determined best reflected the major patterns across all recipes. It could go on to consider all possible consumable items and/or all possible methods that one might be able to use to make the same end product, and then relay those options to the chef.

The selection of inputs, weightings, and data sets determines how useful an AI tool will be, how accurate it can be, and whether it embeds explicit or implicit bias. With regards to a tool designed to predict human behavior, such as the risk assessment tools we will discuss, if the inputs instruct the tool to look for racially identifying characteristics, weigh them heavily, and then use a data set that reflects a community where overpolicing resulted in a disproportionate representation of minorities in the offender population, it is pretty easy to understand how racially skewed results can emerge.

Below, I will walk through some basic aspects of algorithmic design relevant to AI tools. As I proceed, I will be discussing different AI designs—one form that is based on something called *machine learning*, and another form that is not. Both forms of design result in artificially intelligent tools.

Inputs: Selection

AI assessment tools consist of algorithms that have a series of "relevant" inputs — that is, inputs that can help answer a particular question. We can think of the inputs as the factors that matter. In terms of predicting human behavior, the inputs are the aspects of the person that determine or influence his behavior.

For example, when I wake up in the morning, what determines whether I will exercise before or after I have my coffee? To get the most accurate prediction, it would be important to know my exercise history. If I have never exercised in the morning before, the probability that I will today is a lot lower than if I had a regular 6 a.m. routine. Another factor that could provide valuable information would be whether I am in a place that makes exercise easier or harder: whether I am at home, in a hotel, or on an airplane. We might also want to know about my general state of mind with regard to exercise: do I exercise out of guilt, because I am training for a marathon, because my doctor tells me I need to, or for some other reason? And if we wanted to predict the intensity of my exercise, we might need additional information such as my age and health. So, in this example, exercise history, exercise pattern, physical location, state of mind, age, and health could all be inputs.

The question we have posed is the probability that I will exercise before having my morning coffee. For further predictive accuracy, we would also need to have information relating to my coffee consumption. One factor would be: do I even drink coffee? Another factor might be my typical pattern of consumption: do I typically have coffee first thing in the morning, or do I prefer to have it after reading the paper and other activities? Here, my coffee history and pattern of consumption are also inputs.

The selection of inputs that provide information relevant to predicting behavior can occur in several ways. Much of the detail underlying these processes is technical and beyond the scope of my argument. It suffices to broadly highlight three methods of selection. The first allows AI software to parse out the relevant factors itself; this is a form of machine learning, as the machine is designed to teach itself and ideally make itself better and better at a task as it goes. Another method is for humans to select the inputs. A third method is a combination of the first two, with the AI tool arriving at initial selections and humans providing review and adjustments of the inputs (machine learning can include human adjustment of the algorithm, to the extent the human continues to understand it).

Whenever a human is involved in the selection or adjustment of inputs, we must ask on what basis and with what potential biases the human is approaching the selection and adjustment process. Given that there is no master book of correct inputs, it is crucial to understand why a human might have chosen certain inputs and not others. This understanding is necessary, in part, to assess the rationale behind the selections: were the inputs based in reason or on a normative concept of which inputs are relevant, or do they tend toward the personal biases of the selector? But even when the machine is designed to learn inputs itself, the human can instruct it to focus on or ignore certain information — for instance, race, gender, disability, or any other characteristic.

One of the main criticisms of AI tools that predict recidivism is the lack of transparency with regards to inputs that a model uses to arrive at its objective, including the human role in the selection process. Designers have not provided sufficient information about their underlying design choices and the ways in which the inputs for these tools were selected. As we will discuss in later chapters, there are several important, documented instances in which humans have designed what are called "theoretically driven" models that contain inputs based on their own view of relevance rather than a more concrete standard. Unchecked, this could be the beginning of a slippery slope.

There are, however, some typical inputs among tools designed to predict criminal recidivism. Some of the standards are prior criminal history, age of first arrest, current age, highest level of education achieved, marital status, residential status, employment history, substance use, and peer associations.

Several tools also use inputs which encompass vague categories like "antisocial attitude," "resistance to authority," and "cultural predispositions." As is a recurring theme with these tools, we don't have sufficient information in any case to know exactly how these inputs were chosen or altered by humans.

Determination of Input Weights

An input's weight in an algorithm reflects its relative importance to the equation as a whole. For example, if there is only one input in an algorithm, the input's weight would be 100%. In this simple scenario, the input would also be the same as the output. In some algorithms, including in some of the risk assessment tools that are relevant to my argument, there are instances where every input can be given the same weighting.

As with input selection, weightings can be determined in various ways. AI tools with machine learning can be allowed to independently review a data set, like a set of arrest records, and determine what patterns are present in the set and why. The tool can then determine relative weights of the inputs. Another method is to use a form of statistical analysis, like a regression model, to determine the relative importance — that is, weight — of a factor within a prediction. A third method to determine weightings is human selection and adjustment.

As with inputs, there is no industry-wide standard to establish, set, or adjust weightings. Some tools, such as the COMPAS tool and the federal PCRA tool, rely heavily on criminology theory and research to determine both appropriate inputs and weightings. But criminological theories are often hotly debated and are by no means accepted as a normative framework pursuant to which we should design an entire justice system.

There has been no attempt to achieve national consensus as to the value of weightings, nor are there even national standards that set guidelines for the adjustment of weightings. A hypothetical example of such a guideline would be, for instance, a requirement that software designers make any adjustments in weightings based on peer reviewed research, that they disclose the adjustment, and that they overtly identify the adjustments in the code itself.

It would be more than useful to have some sort of standard guidelines for input weightings and adjustments, as these weightings and adjustments can fundamentally alter the outcomes of a behavioral prediction tool. If a human is manually adjusting these weightings, then there is almost no way to tell, at least from an outsider's perspective, if the resulting prediction is more the result of a mathematical process or an arbitrary intervention.

For example, if an AI tool reviews the data for a pattern of criminal behavior and determines that arrests have a very strong correlation with a New York City zip code, then the tool might give that zip code a high weighting. A human might then examine that algorithm, determine that this specific zip code is a proxy for race, and manually lower the weighting to avoid racial impropriety. Maybe this human reviewer made this decision based on the fact that Stop and Frisk practices were prominent in that neighborhood during the time span of the data set. Maybe the human reviewer just made the decision on gut instinct. Regardless of his reasoning, this reviewer might reduce the weight by any chosen percentage, whether it be 75%, 19.2%, or 1%. Perhaps it turns out that the reviewer made a good decision in this instance, because the tool was inadvertently racially biased against Black people and would have provided unjust predictive outcomes. But the weighting decision could have easily gone the other way: maybe the reviewer manually adjusted the weighting for a zip code that he perceived to be too low, resulting in worse predictive outcomes for Black people. The real issue here is that there is no standard policy guiding the altering of input weightings and no transparency within the process, so there is simply no way to know what exactly the human reviewer is doing and why. Is there research that supports a change in weighting for this zip code? Do most criminologists and/or AI designers agree that a weighting change is necessary in this zip code? In this zip code scenario, the reviewer might be acting independently as an agent of good or evil, or he might be acting in line with the larger body of research on the topic. It is impossible to tell the difference.

Until there is transparency with regards to inputs and weightings, or until there is a set of standards, or preferably some form of both, any conclusions that these AI assessment tools yield should rest in the shadow of doubt.

The Selection of Data Sets

The other half of algorithmic logic is data sets, the essential learning tools to which the algorithmic logic is applied. Decision-making surrounding data sets should also be subject to close scrutiny.

The world — everything that we see and do — can be reduced to a functional AI data set. The thought can be alarming: we constantly create records that allow AI to determine our very next move. Any time we engage in an activity that creates a record, like recording a voice memo, making a virtual bank deposit, or inputting a destination on Waze, we have created data that AI can distill into a pattern and use.

Yet, data sets have one enormous limitation: all data within a data set is definitionally a record of something. That means that an event — a walk to the park, the creation of a grocery list, a purchase of marijuana — had to occur and be documented. If there's no inventory of the event, like if you kept the grocery list in your head instead of writing it down, or were not arrested for buying drugs, then, technically, in the world of AI, what you did never occurred. The data within the data set is an accumulation of discrete, documented events; despite the technological wonder of AI, it cannot read recorded data where there is none.

Another common theme recurs: there is no master list with regards to rules and regulations of data sets. There is no set of universal standards in terms of vetting data sets for content or accuracy. Human choice of a data set means that we need to be on the lookout for the possibility of human error or biases in the selection process.

Just as data sets reflect recorded moments in time, they also reflect historical, social, political, and cultural moments. The fact that certain events occurred once does not mean that they will occur again. In the criminal justice area this is particularly important since what constitutes a crime can and has changed over time. Likewise, policing practies continue to change, too.

For example, for years the growing, use, possession, or sale of cannabis has been criminalized at both the state and federal levels. A data set of arrest records from virtually anywhere in the United States from only a few years ago undoubtedly reflects arrests for cannabis-related crimes. Today, though, many states have decriminalized much conduct relating to cannabis. Thus, things for which a person might have been arrested for in the past, like buying a dime bag or smoking a joint in public, are not the same as what he would be arrested for today. Arrest records at a state level may therefore state "criminal" behavior in yesterday's terms, even as they're being used to evaluate conduct today.[3]

Moreover, criminal laws are constantly changing: adultery, gay marriage, the purchase and possession of alcohol, and interracial marriage were all once deemed criminal acts. Likewise, seatbelt laws are relatively new, and the sale of opium and opiates was once far less regulated. A snapshot of a time period reflects the specific criminal laws on the books at that time. We must therefore proceed with great care when extrapolating a data set from one specific time period for universal use in another.

Another caveat to these time snapshots, which only makes this extrapolation more problematic, are changing social conditions. For instance, even before cannabis was officially decriminalized in certain states, arrests for cannabis became far less frequent. Even in today's federal system, while cannabis is still criminalized, authorities expend very few resources on cannabis arrests, instead focusing their efforts on bigger targets. Prostitution is another example of a type of crime in this in-between period: there are fewer and fewer arrests of sex workers for so-called "solicitation" crimes, but, in most places (Nevada being one well-known exception), it has not yet been decriminalized entirely. So, while it would be inaccurate to include an instruction in an AI algorithm to ignore all arrests for charges related to marijuana and solicitation, it is still important to recognize that our social perception of these arrests — the "social weighting" — has changed over time.

New York City's Stop and Frisk policy is a key example in understanding the changing social and political contexts in the creation of data sets. For more than a decade, New York City utilized a crime prevention policing strategy that

---

3   There are, of course, work arounds. For example, an algorithm could be instructed to ignore all cannabis crimes if a designer was particularly concerned about the disparity.

included the "stop, questioning, and frisking" of individuals. The concept was that if police were deployed to certain high-crime neighborhoods, they could prevent crimes from occurring, from being repeated, or from escalating. For some, particularly the Black New Yorkers who this policy disproportionately affected, Stop and Frisk was always a controversial and problematic practice. But the policy didn't really gain significant national attention until 2013, when one of my former judicial colleagues, Judge Shira Scheindlin, deemed it unlawful, ruling that it resulted in racial discrimination.[4] Statistical evidence was presented at the bench trial in front of Judge Scheindlin supporting a claim that there had been significant over-arrest of young Black men from certain neighborhoods during the Stop and Frisk period. There are now various court orders in place that have changed these policing practices in New York City, but the arrest records from that period have not been changed; there are no asterisks on the books. The main implication of this is that a data set of arrest records drawn from the Stop and Frisk period could lead an AI tool to assume that the arrest rates for Black men from this data set are accurate reflections of illegal conduct, when others would argue that most of these arrests never should have occurred, and never would have if the illegal policy had not been in place.

The significance of social and political context is obvious. When AI uses a data set consisting of all arrests for a particular time period in order to predict recidivism for a later point in time, certain arrests which are no longer a crime in that *later period* cannot be predictive of recidivism — at least in the same way. Maintaining a consistent awareness of the time period of any data set is important in assessing the integrity of the AI's conclusions.

There are further issues with data sets. For example, certain data sets can reflect important regional differences. In the United States, this might mean that there is a crime wave particular to a specific place that is not reflective of crimes in other areas.

For example, for years there were locations in Appalachia and parts of the Midwest that saw much higher rates of opioid abuse and related criminal activity than in the rest of the country. As a result, Certain populations in those

---

4   Floyd et al., v. City of New York, 959 F. Supp.2d 540 (S.D.N.Y. 2013).

areas may have criminal records that are incongruent with the criminal picture across the United States. For instance, parts of suburban and rural kentucky may reflect relatively high arrest rates among woman in their mid thirties to mid-forties or among young adults who grew up wealthy. If the designer of an AI tool assumes that the arrest records for opioid-afflicted areas from the early-to-mid 2000s are predictive of nationwide behavior, he might make serious accuracy errors.

Machine learning tools use the data set to iteratively learn what information is important and what patterns within the information reveal. The data set becomes the "world outside" for the tool — it represents the world as it is. Unless instructed otherwise, the AI tool uses the data set to teach it what the world should look like, and the tool's outputs reflect its attempt to recreate the world. Data sets that reflect a world that we no longer view as fair may not be the world we want the tool to rebuild for us again, and again, and again.

Machine Learning and AI Assessment Tools

As I will discuss below, risk assessment is as old as the hills and certainly does not require AI. Humans are perfectly capable of assessing risk for survival — we have done it since prehistoric times. AI allows assessment tools to grapple with far more complex data, to see how different factors interact with one another, and to make predictions. In terms of risk assessment, AI and the machine learning form of AI are now well entrenched. I want to briefly discuss machine learning and these assessment tools to set the stage for later discussions of transparency. The technical details of machine learning are not important, but the black box aspect is.

In 2013, the American Society of Criminology published two articles relating to the use of machine learning in risk assessment in the same issue.[5] In the first,

---

5   R. A. Berk and J. Bleich, "Statistical Procedures for Forecasting Criminal Behavior: A Comparative Assessment", *Criminology & Public Policy*, 12(3) (2013), DOI: 10.1111/1745-9133.12044: and T. Brennan and W. L. Oliver, "The Emergence of Machine Learning Techniques in Criminology", *Criminology & Public Policy*, 12(3) (2013), DOI: 10.1111/1745-9133.12055. Brennan and Oliver were both employees of Northpointe, Inc. (Brennan was a founder), the maker of the most well-known assessment tool, Correctional Offender Management Profiling for Alternative Solutions ("COMPAS")).

Berk and Bleich argued that research supported machine learning's increased accuracy and ability to manipulate complex data needed for criminal risk assessment versus prior statistical methods such as logistic regression.[6] Berk and Bleich warned that while the application of machine learning provided tremendous opportunity in this area:

> [T]he conceptual framework and actual procedures can be very different and require a substantial change in data analysis craft lore. Without a proper appreciation of how the new methods differ from the old, there can be serious operational and interpretive mistakes.[7]

Berk and Bleich discuss one form of machine learning called "random forests" as particularly useful for criminal justice.[8] They acknowledge that this form of AI results in the algorithm becoming a black box.[9]

In their responsive article in the same publication, Brennan and Oliver, designers of assessment tools, discuss the use of random forest machine learning in the criminal justice area with approval.[10] They say "[w]e basically agree with Berk and Bleich on their categorization of what constitutes modern ML [machine learning] methods."[11] They further state that "[w]e agree that RF and several other ML methods have great promise for supporting a wide range of criminal

---

6   A regression analysis is a statistical method used to determine the strength of the relationship between two or more variables. The variable that you want to explain is called the "dependent" variable; and the variable whose relationship to the dependent variable you are trying to understand is called the "explanatory" or "predictor" variable. Thus, for instance, if you wanted to determine the relationship between criminal conduct and age, the offense would be the dependent variable, and age would be the explanatory variable. According to R. A. Berk and J. Bleich, "Statistical Procedures for Forecasting Criminal Behavior: A Comparative Assessment", *Criminology & Public Policy*, 12(3) (2013), "[t]here seems to be no reason for continuing to rely on traditional forecasting tools such as logistic regression" (pp. 1–2), and "adaptive machine learning procedures have the capacity to empirically discover patterns in the data and construct suitably complex decision boundaries" (p. 30).

7   *Ibid.*, p. 4.

8   See *Ibid.*, pp.27–28. I won't go into the details of random forests except to say that it consists of connected "classification trees" that together constitute a "forest". Page 18 of the Berk and Bleich paper describes a random forest design in some detail.

9   *Ibid.*, p. 18.

10 T. Brennan and W. L. Oliver, "The Emergence of Machine Learning Techniques in Criminology", *Criminology & Public Policy*, 12(3) (2013), 551, DOI: 10.1111/1745-9133.12055..

11 *Ibid.*, p. 552.

justice applications."[12] They articulate challenges to "user acceptance" of the use of machine learning.[13] Among such challenges are "the black box problem and practical and political needs to justify criminal justice."[14] Brennan and Oliver understand that machine learning methods may prevent a human from understanding the machine's decision-making process, but argue that this should not prevent use of tools designed with such models:

> Another feature of some ML methods that might hurt acceptance among certain practitioners is that they are not designed to offer any clear logic or explanation for their forecasting decisions. Their logic can be inscrutable to human users, they might be viewed negatively as black box. This failure to offer explanatory tools might be awkward for decision makers who must provide justification for their decisions (e.g. judges, probation officers and parole boards) . . . However, Berk and Bleich (2013) are right to remind us of the differing functions of prediction and explanation and that the goal of ML techniques such as RF [random forest] is limited to forecasting accuracy and this should be the benchmark and not the development of an explanation.[15]

Brennan and Oliver then encourage researchers, such as those at COMPAS, to try machine learning methods.[16] While we do not know precisely when the COMPAS tool first began to use machine learning, we know that it now does.[17]

There is a growing body of literature on what AI methods are, can, and should now be deployed in the risk assessment area.[18]

---

12 *Ibid.*

13 *Ibid.*, pp. 556–558 ("This section discusses possible hurdles that could derail the successful diffusion and productive use of ML methods in criminology and criminal justice", p. 556).

14 *Ibid.*, p. 558.

15 *Ibid.*

16 *Ibid.*, p. 559.

17 COMPAS Practitioner's Guide ("Guide"), p. 13.

18 R. A. Berk and J. M. Hyatt, "Machine Learning Forecasts of Risk to Inform Sentencing Decisions", Federal Sentencing Reporter 27(4) (2015), 222–228, DOI: 10.1525/fsr.2015.27.4.222; C. Wadsworth, F. Vera, and C. Piech, "Achieving Fairness Through Adversarial Learning: An Application to Recidivism Prediction," (2018), arXiv:1807.00199v1 [cs.LG]; S. Tan, J. Adebayo, K. Inkpen, and E. Kamar, "Investigating Human + Machine Complementarity

The bottom line is that AI is used in risk assessment tools, and despite its problems, it's not going anywhere. As of today, there is little transparency as to method, and little transparency as to algorithmic design issues that can embed a variety of biases including inputs, weightings, and data set choices. And these issues feed into a more central one — one that undergirds our criminal justice system: the lack of algorithmic transparency comes into direct conflict with due process considerations, which require that tools used in connection with liberty decisions for an individual be comprehensible and fair.

for Recidivism Predictions", (2018), arXiv:1808.09123v2 [cs.LG]; T. Carlson *et al.*, *Artificial Intelligence in Justice and Public Safety* (IJIS Technology and Architecture Committee, 2019) (www.ijis.org/news/the-itac-releases-white-paper).

Chapter 3

Transparency in Decisions about Human Liberty: The Means to the End *Do* Matter

⚖

s AI risk assessment tools have proliferated, so too have concerns about their transparency. Accordingly, courts are seeing a greater number of cases that challenge the accuracy and/or the potentially discriminatory aspects of algorithms. When these cases were first brought, there were a number of what were cast as "discovery" arguments presented by litigants seeking access to the underlying algorithm itself. Plaintiffs or criminal defendants argued that access to the algorithm would provide them with important information regarding the design of the AI tool, and, in response, the defendants and sometimes an intervening third-party licensor of the AI tool used would argue that the proprietary nature of the algorithm should prevent disclosure.

As a federal judge, I presided over all but a small handful of the discovery disputes that arose in the cases before me. In federal court (with state court analogues) the rules regarding discovery are structured so as to provide broad access to all documentary evidence (including digital evidence) relevant to the issues before the court. It is common to see disputes over the confidential nature of business records. The routine way to deal with confidential material — which again, arises every day — is to use something called a "protective order." A protective order contains provisions typically negotiated by the parties or, if they cannot agree, imposed by the court. It governs who can see what materials and under what conditions. In cases in which there is highly-sensitive material, the answer is not to allow a litigant to keep it under lock and key, but rather to strengthen the protective conditions. Except in a single criminal case involving terrorism and state secrets, I never presided over a case in which the mere commercial sensitivity of material could not be addressed. Nor did I have more than a handful of issues brought to me in which parties failed to comply with these court orders.

A more significant concern that is now being discussed — even by those asserting bias or discriminatory outcomes resulting from an AI tool, is that the algorithms have become so complex, and the way in which machine learning can occur so opaque, that even were a litigant or interest to gain access to the algorithm, the content would be inscrutable, rendering access meaningless. As I outlined in Chapter 2, machine learning techniques are being used today in risk assessment tools, and they are known to be black boxes.[1] According to this line of thought, what matters is not how an AI tool reaches any given decision, but only whether the output of the tool is acceptable. I strongly disagree.

Critical information is contained within algorithms used in the criminal justice arena — information that a plaintiff or a criminal defendant can and should be entitled to, particularly when the algorithm has the potential to affect his liberty. As an initial matter, as we've already discussed, not all algorithms are the same. We also know that humans have the ability to select, deselect, or influence what factors an algorithm includes as inputs, and that humans can adjust weightings. As we will see in our discussion of AI risk assessment tools, the designers of one of the leading tools (Northpointe, for its COMPAS software suite), concede and even advertise as positive their influence in COMPAS's input choices. Thus, examination of algorithms can reveal instances in which, for instance, a company included an input intentionally, intentionally deleted one, or intentionally sought to change a weighting.

The difference that a particular input or weighting of that input may make in the output can be slight, but it is real. For instance, a slight difference could result in a risk score shifting a defendant from a numerical

---

1   See, e.g., R. Berk and J. Bleich, "Statistical Procedures for Forecasting Criminal Behavior: A Comparative Assessment", *American Society of Criminology, Criminology & Public Policy*, 12(3), (2013) and T. Brennan and W. L. Oliver, "The Emergence of Machine Learning Techniques in Criminology," *Criminology & Public Policy*, 12(3) (2013).

score that moves him from low to moderate risk. That difference could dictate whether a defendant spends months or a year in jail awaiting trial or is allowed to remain free until his trial date. This is how quickly and imperceptibly an algorithm, or an algorithm's designer, can irreversibly affect a defendant's life.

Depending on the nature of the case, choices about weightings and inputs could also support or undercut a claim of intentional discrimination. While it is always challenging to find direct evidence of intentional actions that lead to discriminatory impact, an algorithm might provide some fingerprints. Moreover, what's in (and out) of a data set can matter a great deal. Whether a data set covers the correct time period, whether it captures regional variation, and whether it embeds policy choices that led to inflation in certain representations will all impact the results.

In a criminal matter, access to the algorithm and underlying data set could enable a defendant to make arguments regarding a risk assessment that he could not otherwise make or make as effectively: (1) was race included as an input?; (2) were proxies for race included, such as residential zip code or educational institutions?; (3) was the defendant's risk score increased because the data set was drawn from a region or area with demographic differences from that of the defendant? Transparency in the algorithm might provide a measure of justice to a criminal defendant about whom the algorithm is generating predictions.

There are also important ethical reasons for which disclosure of the algorithm matters, mainly that the means used to get to an end matter, particularly when liberty decisions are at stake. Those who argue that the algorithm is irrelevant and that AI tools should be measured by outputs alone are framing the tools as strictly utilitarian — that the ends justify the means. Applied in the criminal justice area, that concept is deeply troubling.

There are also essential fairness issues about the "how" of the AI tools. Do we care if race is used as a predictor of risk assessment if the output is arguably racially neutral? If racial bias is included in an algorithm, might we not care a great deal about that, regardless of the accuracy of the output? Are we not fairly certain that if racial bias has made its way into the algorithm, the output lacks essential integrity?

Certain uses of the output of AI tools are just too important to allow transparency to fall by the wayside. Perhaps one day our methods for analyzing large data sets to make predictions of human behavior will require complex machine learning methods and neural networks beyond human comprehension. If there has been sufficient historical transparency to develop trust in both the accuracy and fairness of AI tools, we may well accept that state of affairs. But that trust is not easily given when accuracy rates are only fair to middling and where fairness and accuracy still clearly diverge.

Now, before the technology has reached that tipping point, is the time to require transparency. Europe has begun to set an example: Article 22 of the General Data Privacy Regulation ("GDPR"), which went into effect in Europe in 2018, provides that individuals subject to a decision based on profiling have the right to the logic of the decision making.[2] The designer is required to implement suitable measures to protect that right.

Regardless of the speed at which the technology is growing more complex, there is no doubt that we can require that certain aspects of any algorithm be transparent. This may impact design choices, like requiring that certain opaque machine learning techniques not be used in the risk assessment area. For many algorithm choices, it is technically feasible for designers to ensure that whatever inputs have been selected or deselected, weightings have been applied, or adjustments made to those weightings, that they all be captured and retained in the code; humans can then review them. The data set that is used is even easier to identify. We can and must insist on this transparency.[3] The means to the end matter, and we cannot and should not give up on accessing the means.

---

2 EU GDR, Art. 22.

3 See C. Rudin, C. Wang, and B. Coker, *The Age of Secrecy and Unfairness in Recidivism Prediction*, *HDSR* (2020), https://doi.org/10.1162/99608f92.6ed64b30.

Chapter 4
Decision-Making: The Human as Case Study

⚖️

I n this chapter, I'm going to put AI up to the mirror of the human brain. How do humans make fair and just decisions? What kinds of errors are embedded in human decision-making? Are we in fact any more accurate than AI — and, if not, are we satisfied that AI has an error rate that is no greater than that of humans?

In addressing these questions, I use an example with which I am personally familiar: how humans make decisions in the criminal justice area. This type of decision-making is heavily value laden and requires one human's assessment of another. As part of this discussion, I will lay out my view of how ethical and value-based frameworks are infused throughout human decision-making. Next chapter, I will undertake a similar exercise for AI tools: how do they incorporate aspects of ethical and value frameworks in their design and through the data sets upon which they are so reliant?

The Human Decision-Making Process

Humans make decisions based on a combination of random guesswork, intuition, rule-based belief systems, ethical frameworks, cultural or social norms, associations or biases, and data. We use our accumulated experience and wisdom to form judgments that help us with our decisions. In short, we make decisions based on the constellation of facts that makes us an individual.

The degree of incorrectness in human decision-making can reflect errors in any one of the domains we use to make a decision: perhaps we made a random guess and it was wrong; or we made an assumption that turned out to be false, in whole or in part; or perhaps we brought personal bias into the decision-making. Maybe the data we relied upon was imperfect in some way. After all, when humans make decisions we rarely have access to "perfect" data. Adding further complexity, every fact that we learn occurs within a specific historical context. Our data sets are thus tethered to history in ways that are analogous to the data sets we present to AI tools.

Predictions about human behavior may be particularly fraught with error. Consider first impressions: how many times have you misjudged someone who later proved you wrong — like a coworker who you thought was shy but actually loves small talk? And consider how frequently people surprise us: even though your friend had been talking about moving to California for three years, did you actually think he was gong to do it? As much as we like to hope otherwise — and implement rigorous vetting processes to protect against surprises — it's difficult to say with certainty that judges are any better than the rest of us at predicting human behavior. Even judges whose decisions may be considered "correct" most frequently (based, perhaps, on the number of appellate reversals) still don't get it "right" all the time. Judges are fallible, too.

As a judge, I made thousands of decisions. For each decision I was asked to make, of course I endeavored to make the "right" one. I combined my accumulated experience with the facts as I understood them, and I tried to be attentive to predispositions or biases that I might have. Nevertheless, I sometimes erred.

Some decisions took place at the outset of a particular case: what's the right schedule for this case? How quickly should the parties have to reach certain milestones? Should bail be granted? Were there terms of release for a criminal defendant that would increase the likelihood that he would show up for future court appearances and also ensure an appropriate level of safety to the community? I made decisions about whether certain evidence should be exchanged between parties, whether evidence should come in or be precluded, and whether a civil case could be resolved without a trial.

If a defendant was convicted of a crime, I made decisions about whether he should be jailed immediately ("remanded" is the legal term), if he should serve prison time for the crime, and, if so, for how long and under what conditions. I tried to exercise the best judgment I had based upon the information known to me. Many times, parties in a case did not agree with my decisions. These disagreements were expressed in the form of verbal or non-verbal conduct in the courtroom, motions to reconsider a ruling, or an appeal.

Each of the decisions — from the big to the small — required me to exercise discretion. Discretion is judgment based on rational consideration of the law, reason, and experience. In the United States, our system of common law requires judges to exercise their personal discretion when considering how to proceed. For instance, even in what might seem to be a routine area like schedule setting, consideration of a number of factors is required in order to set both a fair and reasonable schedule for all parties — a schedule that is too aggressive or too slow might result in a real unfairness to one side or the other. As a judge, I needed to balance all the factors of a case and consider the complexity of preparing for trial — certain cases might require more witnesses or documents than others. I also needed to look at whether an individual case needed to be resolved on a particular schedule in order to provide adequate relief to a party. An employment dispute left open, for example, might cast a shadow on an individual's career. So too a copyright case in which alleged infringement might result in the dilution of a market opportunity; a maritime case in which a ship or its cargo are at issue might be held in port, impacting the next delivery; or a pharmaceutical patent case that prevents or delays a potentially important drug from being released into the market. I also considered the financial circumstances of the parties: delays in the schedule might be tolerable to one party but might result in insurmountable attorney's fees for another. Parties would often present dueling arguments to me and I would question them about their rationale, judge the merits of their arguments, and assess their credibility.

Those were the "simple" decisions. More complicated decisions might involve whether evidence should be admitted — judicial discretion plays a role here, too. For instance, judges routinely make decisions as to whether an otherwise admissible piece of evidence should be excluded on the basis that its probative value is substantially outweighed by the danger of unfair prejudice, confusion of the issues, misleading the jury, or wasting time.

31

These decisions are called "403 determinations," based on the Federal Rule of Evidence that corresponds with this rule. To make a proper "403 determination," judges engage in a balancing exercise. Sometimes "403 issues" present close or complicated cases for a judge to analyze. For example, if a defendant is an alleged terrorist who is on trial for a crime involving explosives, would showing a jury a video of that defendant speaking frequently in the past about the use of explosives be more likely to demonstrate lack of mistake (a proper purpose for the use of such evidence), or to suggest specific guilt in this particular instance (an improper purpose)? Each decision that I made like this required my judgment, discretion, and experience.

Morality and Fairness in Human Decision-Making

Judicial decision-making, like all human decision-making, is infused with concepts of fairness and morality. When making a decision, some facts may be given little weight, and others more. This weighing of facts entails assessments of importance and prioritization that often reflect an individual's ethical framework.

As an example, let us consider a bail determination. When I was making a decision about whether to release someone on bail or to deny bail and incarcerate him immediately, I weighed a number of facts. First, I weighed the nature of the crime and its seriousness. Some crimes are plainly serious — crimes that result in death, robbery at gunpoint, or certain drug crimes, such as trafficking in 10 kilos of cocaine. Other crimes may not be serious in quite the same way, such as a drug crime of trafficking in a 1/2 kilo of marijuana when many states have already legalized recreational use. This is a crime, but is it a *serious* one? What about a fraud involving the creation and cashing of $4000 of fake gift cards? What about someone who was previously convicted of a felony, served time, and then gets caught with a gun in the glove compartment of his car? He says he only had the gun because he lives in a gang-infested area and needs protection — is that a serious crime? Some would think so. Judges are scattered across the country and come from a variety of different communities and personal backgrounds. They have demonstrably and widely varying views on how they perceive the seriousness of a crime — drug crimes, in particular, are perceived as vastly different from community to community.

My belief was that drug crimes that did not involve weapons could nonetheless be serious and dangerous, even when the crime itself might involve a relatively small quantity. It depended on the facts. My position was based on a belief that drugs tear apart families and communities; that selling addictive drugs into communities means that kids become addicted and build the market; that parents become desperate and spend money they could be using for food, clothing, and shelter for their children on drugs instead; and that addiction can lead to additional crimes, including crimes of violence. I did not believe that drug crimes are "victimless." Some judges agree with that view; some do not.

The next step in a bail decision was to weigh the strength of the evidence, based on representations ("proffers") made by the Assistant US Attorneys. I would consider what the proffer was with regard to wires, eyewitness evidence, documents, video, cooperating testimony, or an FBI agent's statements about what had been seized as part of executing on a search warrant. Needless to say, some cases look strong to one set of eyes and not as strong to another; while some cases are clearly supported by overwhelming evidence, others are based on untested theories and largely circumstantial evidence. Assessing the strength of the evidence depends in part on who is making the proffer and the judge's experience with the credibility of that person — over time, a judge will form impressions of many of the "repeat players" in the legal system, such as the Assistant US Attorneys or District Attorneys, as well as members of law enforcement.

After assessing the strength of the evidence, I would assess the likelihood that the defendant would appear in court when scheduled to do so. I would weigh the person's family obligations, his connections to his community, the severity of the penalty he was facing, his prior criminal history, and his prior history of being a no-show for court appearances. I would also consider whether there were particular reasons why a defendant's prior history might not be indicative of his present tendencies — perhaps he had a new girlfriend who was helping him to get his life together, a new child, or a new job. The defendant might address me during a bail hearing and tell me why I should not remand him and what kind of personal commitment he would make to showing up to all of his hearings.

Then, based on of all the facts in front of me, I would make a decision about whether the person was a good bail risk. In making this decision, I relied on my value system to lead me in the direction of what I thought was the best and most just decision. Sometimes the answer would be less-complicated: in a gang-related drug crime I might deny bail for everyone in a large group of similarly-situated defendants. But sometimes the determinations were more ambiguous. How should I assess a young man who had already served time for one drug crime, was released and had a lawful job, but then was arrested for a minor possession crime? The fact pattern or the Guidelines might suggest incarceration, but my value system or instincts might guide me in the opposite direction; it's rarely clear-cut.

I made bail determinations for more people than I can count. They resulted in real consequences if I got them wrong. If a defendant was a danger to his community, I risked the safety of potential victims. If he was not — either because he was not in fact guilty, or because his behavior had been truly aberrant — I risked potential harm — economic, psychological, and social — to a defendant incarcerated for a lengthy pre-trial period. Each bail determination was unique. Each and every one required me to assess a human being's life story and make a judgment about his character and relevant circumstances.

While bail determinations could be difficult, I made much harder decisions as a judge. Sentencings were among the hardest. When making a decision about whether to incarcerate a defendant for a crime and how long, I undertook a similar analysis to the bail determination I have just described. But a sentencing decision carried an additional burden: it could deprive another human being of his liberty for years or even the rest of his life.

To make a sentencing decision, I would carefully consider the facts of the now-established criminal conduct; once again, my personal values and ethical framework played a very significant role. And yet, despite every attempt, to be as fair as possible, it's impossible to ignore the fact that differences between judges' values and ethical frameworks can result in differing outcomes for even similarly-situated defendants.

Variability in Human Decision-Making

I considered myself a very thoughtful, careful sentencer. But I also understood that my sentence for a particular person might be different from that which a judge sitting next door to me might give to the same person for the same crime. I understood that as hard as I tried to get it right, and as hard as the judge next door to me tried to get it right, our sentences might vary. And in that variability resided potential unfairness.

When making a sentencing decision, I spent significant time repeatedly reading all materials provided to me. I always considered multiple time frames as potential sentences and would ask myself whether a time period that might initially seem appropriate was too long, or why one a month shorter sentence would not serve the same purposes perfectly well.

Each summer, I read the last several dozen sentencing transcripts of every judge in my federal judicial district, the Southern District of New York. I read these to gain insight into whether we differed significantly in our understanding of the nature of criminal behavior and what constituted an appropriate punishment. Reading the transcripts of judges that I encountered on a regular basis and whose dockets of randomly-assigned cases were generally the same as mine taught me first and foremost that sentencing differentials exist and persist amongst judges who sit next door to each other and regardless of political affiliation. I learned that there was great variability even among judges who sat in the same district and saw the same types of cases. I was considered a "law and order" judge — one who imposed sentences more consistently within the Federal Sentencing Guidelines than not. National statistics for my district showed that some of my fellow judges sentenced below the Guidelines, and, every once in a while, a few went above.

I also regularly compared the sentences imposed within the Southern District of New York to those imposed in other districts around the country. The Federal

Judicial Center keeps a broad array of statistics relating to sentencing that are publicly available. The differentials with which I was familiar in my district were only a small piece of a much more complicated picture: there can be wide variations in sentencing from district to district across the country.

People have long recognized the reality of and unfairness in sentencing differentials. In 1987, the US Congress first adopted the Federal Sentencing Guidelines as an explicit attempt to try and reduce sentencing disparities both between judges and between districts. For a period of almost a decade, judges were required to sentence defendants within a range of months established for particular crimes. Then, in 2005, the Supreme Court determined that it was unconstitutional for the Guidelines to be mandatory. Since then, Supreme Court case law requires that every judge begin a sentencing proceeding by correctly calculating a Guidelines range, and then stating whether he is sentencing within it or varying from it. Appeals from sentences that have been imposed in a procedurally appropriate manner are given significant deference by the appellate courts.

In sum, there are more than 600 district court judges and thousands of state court judges imposing sentences every day — all of those sentences are in some way unique. As I peviously discussed, not every judge views crimes similarly. For some, one type of crime may be considered more serious than another. The statutory requirements for sentencing impose a discipline upon judges, but even those are subject to wide variability. For example, a primary statutory requirement for any judge making a sentencing decision is to consider the seriousness of the offense, leaving that consideration up to the discretion of the judge.

A second statutorily required consideration is whether a particular sentence will achieve the purposes of sentencing: is a sentence designed to achieve rehabilitation, "just deserts" or retribution, to incapacitate, to deter, or something else?

Not surprisingly, judges differ on their views as to whether any period of incarceration can achieve all of these purposes. For instance, some judges view incarceration as entirely inconsistent with rehabilitation. For me, it depended on whether I thought that a period of incarceration would assist in convincing a defendant that life on the inside was sufficiently unpleasant to make criminal behavior not worth it. There are judges who view retribution as a rare basis for incarcerating someone. My own view was that retributive punishment can be critical to living within an ordered society, in which we have established a set of laws that cannot be broken without consequence, lest we risk a slide into anarchy.

Humans: Doing the Best We Can

What we want most from human decision-making in the criminal justice area is a rational and reasoned process, grounded in law. As discussed at length, there is no single way in which judges make decisions, and there is no single value system. Rather, judicial decisions are currently made by people drawn from every walk of life, with varied backgrounds, cultural traditions, and ethical frameworks.

The law imposes certain disciplines onto that heterogenous group. It requires that decisions implicating human liberty be stated clearly on the written record. A judge must set forth in a transcribed hearing, or in a written decision, the reasons for his or her decision. From practice, we know that some judges say more and others less when satisfying this mandate. The written record provides a basis for an appeal of the decision to a higher court — another panel of human judges who are tasked with determining if the decision fell within acceptable substantive and procedural parameters. Variability among judges is accepted as a result of the differences between us all, but fairness according to the standards set forth in the US Constitution and relevant case law is nonetheless required.

Crucially, all the decisions judges make are *individual* decisions based on their individual experiences about individual human beings' liberty. There is no "group" sentencing, nor any "group" liberty decisions. In the realm of human judicial decision-making, we have all agreed that the Constitution requires more.

Chapter 5
Decision-Making: AI as Case Study

⚖️

I n previous chapters, we considered ways in which decision-making involving liberty decisions embeds the value systems of the decider. Decisions that involve human discretion necessarily involve the application of judgment based in part on the personal characteristics of the decision-maker. As AI tools become increasingly involved in making some of the same decisions that humans have historically made, we should not expect the outcomes to suddenly attain a type of consistency that human decision-making lacks. Nor should we expect that when AI tools make decisions that we typically associate with human value systems that the AI tools do not call upon similar value systems. Instead, we must first look at how AI tools embed value systems, then ask whether humans are doing enough to ensure that the tools reflect values that will result in fairness at an individual level.

The area of risk assessment provides us with a nearly direct — and therefore particularly useful — comparison between different decision-making processes: the output of any given risk assessment, whether determined by an AI technology or a human, necessarily correlates to a real-life human outcome. And so as we weigh the benefits of human versus machine, we must ask ourselves: are AI tools more effective than humans — which is to say: more accurate, more efficient, more ethically consistent — in making liberty decisions?

When Do AI Tools Use Value Systems

AI tools are now able to accomplish a wide variety of tasks. There are tools for facial and voice recognition, language translation, autonomous vehicle operation, medical diagnostic, financial management, inventory management, product development and manufacturing, and — of course — tools that assess risk and needs for criminal offenders. Not by a long stretch do all of these tools involve decision-making that calls on a value system. Many of them do not require the exercise of judgment or discretion in the human sense. Whether or not AI tools use value systems in decision-making depends chiefly on the type of task they are tasked to perform.

Certain AI tools are tasked with making "objectively binary" decisions. That is, a tool is asked to perform a task to which there is an objective right or wrong answer; with perfect information, whether the tool gets it "right" can be tested and known. When AI is making decisions in this area, it need not call upon a value system or ethical framework, because there are no values or ethics embedded within its decision. An easy example of this binary decision-making would be an AI tool that assists radiologists with identifying malignant tumors. The tumor is either malignant or not, and AI operating upon perfect information would reveal that. While an AI tool may be exercising judgment — for instance, to decide whether it is more likely than not that a particular mass has malignant characteristics — no one would credibly argue that value systems play a role in this decision. So too with AI decision-making involving facial and voice recognition. Here again, with perfect information, there is a right or wrong answer: it's either your face and voice, or it's not.

With some tools, though, "objectively binary" decisions can easily become muddled. Autonomous vehicles are a good example. These vehicles are mostly tasked with binary decisions: stop at a light, adhere to a speed limit, follow a street sign. But what happens when a human actor — a child, perhaps, who has run into the street — interferes with this binary clockwork?

Let's quickly reconsider the trolley problem, which was outlined in Chapter One. All versions of the trolley problem require a rendering of judgment: keep the trolley on the first track or switch to the second. And all of these judgments, no matter the iteration of the trolley problem, require an ethical determination on harm: run over one person or group, or run over the person or group on the other track. And so, on some level, the problem always boils down to an essential juxtaposition: is definitive action that results in an intentional killing worse than passivity that results in death?

An autonomous car is following a speed limit of twenty-five miles-per-hour on a residential road when, suddenly, a child jumps into its path. The vehicle senses that the child is in its path and has enough time to swerve out of the way, if it so chooses. However, if it swerves, it will hit, and likely kill, an elderly couple on the sidewalk. What should the autonomous vehicle do? As of yet, there is no clear-cut answer on this real-life trolley problem; companies that manufacture autonomous vehicles are laboring over this decision as I write. Whatever they do decide — which is to say, whatever the human manufacturers decide to instruct their AI technology — it is certain that the resolution will reflect an ethical framework that may vary from person-to-person and company-to-company.

AI Tools and Liberty Decisions

AI tools that assist in liberty determinations fall squarely into the category of non-binary decision-makers. These liberty decisions require discretion and judgment that implicate ethical and value systems; there is no "right" answer. Often when I speak about AI tools, audiences are surprised to learn that the predictions they make are not somehow purely objective and that there are value systems embedded in AI tools, either explicitly or implicitly. Some listeners resist this idea, arguing that these tools have a "value-neutral" design. My answer is that what we call "value-neutral" is not necessarily neutral at all.

There are several ways in which AI tools that engage in discretionary decision-making can intentionally or inadvertently include human value systems in the design. This can occur in a straightforward way: inputs into the algorithm can be selected or deselected in ways that reflect a human's values. Does the human believe that race is an input relevant to assessment of the likelihood of recidivism? If race is deselected, are proxies for race (neighborhood, school attended, age at first arrest) nonetheless allowed? How are weightings to inputs assigned or adjusted? The importance of design choices as a mechanism for the conveyance of human values comes up in later chapters as we discuss specific risk assessment tools, so it is worth a preparatory in-depth discussion now.

Value Systems and Ethics *Within the Design*

There are several ways in which design choices can embed value systems, but a critically important starting point is the articulation of the task the AI is asked to perform. In many cases, the nature of the decision the AI is being asked to make can itself embed a value system or ethical framework. Thus, while we often think of the tasks we ask AI to accomplish as being "value neutral," the very design of the task can itself be laden with a theoretical perspective. For instance, if we ask an AI tool to assist us with "what criminal justice sentence would best achieve rehabilitation?" or "what sentence would reflect the seriousness of the offense?" the tasks themselves posit sentencing goals.

An AI tool designed with the objective of predicting the sentence that would be most likely to achieve rehabilitation suggests a value system prioritizing reintegration into society. In contrast, a tool designed to predict a sentence that achieves retribution — an imposition of penalties for breaking the social code — may result in longer periods of incarceration and far less focus on reintegration.

It is fair to ask whether anyone really develops AI tools that set out to achieve these specific goals. In other words, does anyone ever design an AI tool with "rehabilitation" or "retribution" as the primary goal or are they merely asking AI to assess patterns and make basic statistical calculations? Let us assume for the moment that a designer intends to develop a software tool that does just that: it "simply" reviews prior sentencing data in order to "answer the question" of what kinds of sentences are more likely to result in reduced criminal conduct in the long term. In other words, the AI tool is tasked by the human designer with examining outcomes of criminal behavior ("this resulted in more crime," or "this resulted in less") and looking at the characteristics (including types of sentences imposed) that achieved those results. But this choice — the articulation of a task as an assessment of patterns that resulted in an outcome framed as "more versus less crime" — is, in and of itself, asking a value-based question.

The framing of the question de-emphasizes other potential patterns the data might reveal and therefore influences the uses to which it is put. For instance, another framing could emphasize rehabilitation over incarceration, with a task articulation of "assess patterns that resulted in the defendants being less likely (or, more likely) to successfully reintegrate into society." In short, the objective of the AI tool can implicitly frame the way in which the data is looked at and used — it can be heavily value laden.

A second way in which design choices can embed value systems is the selection of inputs. To the extent that a human is choosing one or more of the inputs, those inputs can reflect the human designer's own view as to what kinds of characteristics are important. There are many people who would view the inclusion of race as an input in predicting violent behavior as inherently racist. They might agree that an "objective" assessment of a data set suggests race as an appropriate input, but caution that the structural inequalities, leading to many arrests unvoidably infect the data set with racial bias. A decision to eliminate race as an input altogether is certainly a choice one could make, but is it the right choice? Are we able to achieve a national or even regional consensus on whether to include or exclude race as an input? If it is excluded manually, then are other potential race proxies — such as a residential zip code — also excluded? Most importantly, who is making these decisions and based on what information?

A final area in which design can embed human value systems is in the weightings assigned to various inputs. As discussed more thoroughly in Chapter 2, weighting adjustments can easily reflect the human's view of how important an input is, or whether the input needs to be removed altogether (and thus the weighting brought to zero). But upon what are those views based? It could be anything from a personal opinion, to a social science consensus, to direction from a supervising body.

Again using race as an example in the criminal justice area, an AI tool reviewing a data set of historical arrests might find a pattern suggesting that race is a highly correlated characteristic, and thus weigh race heavily in its predictions of criminality. The human designer, reviewing the inputs and weightings derived by the AI tool, might feel he needs to "correct" and manually reduce that weighting, as he has deemed it reflective of racist policies that resulted in the over-arrest of minorities. This determination, and the subsequent adjustment to some other level (including potentially zero), would necessarily be based on views that are unlikely subject to immediate universal agreement. That is, not everyone would agree that the algorithm should be adjusted at all, or, if so, by how much.

All of this means that at each level of design of an AI tool — the questions posed, the inputs chosen, and the weightings assigned — human value systems have the opportunity to announce and embed themselves within the design.

Value Systems and Ethics *Within the Data*

We have already discussed that the choice of the appropriate data set is critical to AI's efficacy. A data set from a different time period or region may teach an AI tool things about crime that at least some people would no longer believe to be true. The recent decriminalization of marijuana in some states and changing societal attitudes toward sex work are good examples of this.

But beyond that, each data set represents of aggregation of *data points*. Those data points themselves reflect decisions that at one time required the exercise of some amount of individual discretion or judgment. The data points, then, are actual reflections of a human decision-maker's value system and ethical framework.

Let me take this in smaller steps, and we will use some criminal justice examples to make the points clearly. As we discussed in Chapter 4, all judges bring their own value systems and ethical frameworks with them to work each day. Each decision they make about a defendant's character, his prospects for rehabilitation, and his propensities as a person generally reflect those values. As a result, a data set that contains the data related to that decision ("this person, with the following characteristics, was sentenced to 23 months for the following crime"), is inflected with data points that embed the value system of the decision-makers. The data set is, in essence, a collection of individualized decision-making.

When AI learns from a data set, the information it captures includes not only factual information (the age of the defendant, race, marital status, educational history), but also judgments about how different types of crimes are viewed (arrested or not arrested, denied bail or granted bail, sentenced to x amount of time or y amount of time). All of these data points reflect decisions made by different people, with different lifestyles, different cultural backgrounds, and potentially quite different value systems and ethical frameworks.

Of course, there is an argument that aggregation of a vast quantity of data smooths out these individual differences. There are several reasons why this is an inadequate explanation. First, we have no indication that these data sets are being drawn in a truly randomized manner. Without complete transparency into the underlying data set, we cannot know whether it is disproportionately drawn from certain jurisdictions with certain judges. In some jurisdictions there are only a handful of judges; a data set drawn from such a jurisdiction would therefore necessarily reflect decision-making by only a few. In addition, even if the data set was drawn from many jurisdictions, there are certain judges who make a disproportionate number of sentences within a jurisdiction. I was one such judge — I would sentence my defendants relatively quickly and took on sentencing over 100 defendants for other judges. As a result, a snapshot of the database drawn from the period when I was a judge might reflect a disproportionate number of my sentences. This is undoubtedly the case as well in other areas of the country and at other times.

Evaluating "Accuracy"

There are clear perils in using AI tools that are making decisions based on unexpected or unshared value systems and ethical frameworks. I have discussed instances in which changing notions of what constitutes criminal behavior can lead to misleading data sets that purport to reflect "crimes." I have also referenced regional community differences that can make the use of a data set drawn from one community less useful or affirmatively unfair, in connection with decision-making about a person from an entirely different community. For instance, there was a time while Georgia had criminalized gay relationships that New York City was hosting gay pride parades. Other regional differences persist and have meaning for the fair application of AI tools.

As of this date, there are no rules or regulations that require companies developing AI risk and analysis tools to standardize or regionalize the use of data sets. What this means on a practical level is that an AI tool could be trained on a data set drawn from Georgia and used to predict recidivism or violence in New York City, or elsewhere. This current lack of regulation carries a host of perils. First and most obviously, the data set may generally reflect crimes and characteristics of defendants more specific to one place — like an opioid or crack scourge that resulted in a highly community-specific crime wave. Less obviously, but as importantly, the decision-making that underlies the arrest and sentencing data will also reflect the value systems specific to the judge or arresting officer. Do we think the value systems are the same in NYC as in Georgia? Close enough? Too far? For these reasons, there are unpredictable perils for all involved when using an AI tool without full transparency into the data set.

This is not to say that the companies developing AI tools for the criminal justice system are not attempting to ensure accuracy. Reports written about tool design reflect that designers often spend significant time trying to get the data training set just right; They do test for "accuracy." But designers do not control where the software is licensed and deployed. Some tools explicitly disclose that they can be calibrated by jurisdiction. Others are silent on this topic.

Additionally, "accuracy" can be a flexible term; AI tools do not guarantee, they predict. AI risk assessment tools predict that someone *is likely to* commit a crime based on a series of characteristics drawn from patterns in the data set; the tools do not guarantee that he *will* commit any crime. There is also a margin of error — the algorithm will never achieve 100% accuracy with its predictions. Nor, of course, will humans. Which should we accept: Human error based on potentially good intentions, or machine error based on no intentions at all?

Utilitarian by Nature

On a macro level — putting aside the individual value systems that may be embedded throughout an AI tool's design and training — the usage of AI tools in the criminal justice system reflects a clear value system: utilitarianism. AI risk assessment tools are utilitarian both in design and purpose.

These tools make predictions — rooted in the behavior of the majority — about an individual's conduct and relationship to the society he inhabits. When an AI tool predicts that an individual's pre-trial incarceration will benefit society at-large, it is prioritizing the welfare of the majority; that is a classically utilitarian calculation. What makes this whole process even more troubling, and even more pointedly utilitarian, is the inaccuracy of the predictions.

To make its predictions about an individual, the AI uses patterns it has extrapolated from the data set's majority behavior. While using information regarding average outcomes to predict a future outcome is common, perhaps it is ill-suited to the criminal risk assessment context, where the stakes are much higher than a common application. As you can likely gather from this process of rough averages, AI risk assessment tools are often wrong — about 30% of the time, in fact. That life-altering liberty decisions can be based on faulty tools reveals two truths: that the designers and licensors of these tools have prioritized certain alleged efficiencies over fairness, and that they implicitly rely on utilitarian principles.

It nearly goes without saying that all of this — the design of these tools, their applications, and so forth — plays a role in perpetuating systems of structural inequality. It is understood that AI tools deliver the harshest and least fair predictions to Black defendants.

Some may argue that human judges are no better; this is a worthwhile objection. But, at the very least, we hope and expect that human arbiters strive for fairness and accuracy in every decision they make. This is not to say that all humans are good, or well-motivated, or even that they're always right, but that to completely remove the humanity from the situation — the *desire* to be right 100% of the time — is to lay down in front of our Constitution and admit defeat. We cannot allow 70% accuracy to be the standard. Where would we go from there?

Chapter 6
As Old as the Hills: When Humans Assess Risk

⚖

The exercise of trying to predict risk is nothing new. The first risk assessment tool was the human mind. We assessed the risk of crossing the land mass stretched endlessly in front of us. We assessed the risk that the humans in territory in which we wanted to hunt would be friendly or rapacious. Moreover, humans have been assessing the risk of suspected or actual criminal behavior for as long as criminal conduct has been occurring — which is to say, forever. What is new is having machines do it for us, and expecting less in the way of fairness.

There is a growing usage of AI tools to assess risk using "scientific" and "evidence-based" methodologies, and a corresponding belief that such assessments produce results that are both more objective and more accurate than humans can produce. Today, despite the proliferation of risk assessment software tools and due to the number of situations in which risk must be assessed, human-directed assessments remain predominant. Every day, law enforcement responds to incidents without the benefit of tools that provide them with predictions of what is likely to occur: will the incident escalate, will the suspect flee, will there be violence?[1] Human judgment — with all of the wisdom, instinct and imperfections it can bring to bear — largely informs the response. While certain

---

1 Certain AI tools are beginning to be deployed in these areas, but their usage is still nascent. New York City's Domain Awareness System (DAS) is a version of such a tool. DAS combines vast quantities of data (text, audio, video, statistical), from databases throughout New York City; it also collects live and historic video footage from cameras in bridges, poles, and police vehicles. DAS synthesizes this information faster and more completely than any human could, and can provide officers on the street with information relating to a person or residence including the mental health, drug abuse of domestic violence history of residents, whether a resident has been arrested before, has served time, has outstanding warrants, is on a target or search list, and more.

AI-enabled tools have already been deployed in some metropolitan areas to assist with the initial response to potential incidents, such tools have not been deployed in most of the country. As of now, fast moving events with unexpected developments continue to necessitate the use of human judgment as the primary risk assessment tool and response planner.

Similarly, before the use of AI risk assessment tools, pre-trial officers, judges, or prison personnel based their assessments on accumulated experience, information gathered through interviews and interactions, and judgment. This now old-fashioned form of human assessment is referred to in the literature as "clinical judgment."

The Goal of Risk Assessment

To help ward off the potential for arbitrarily-based liberty decisions, we have long sought to create tools that are "evidence based." The first risk assessment tools were simple statistical calculations of perceived risk factors performed by hand, calculator, and later computer. The hope was to develop a way of more accurately determining the needs of both the community and the individual defendant.

A major milestone in the move towards "evidence based" decision-making was the development of the federal Sentencing Guidelines (the "Guidelines"), first rolled out in November 1987. As discussed in Chapter Four, the creation of the Guidelines represented an attempt to limit the breadth of sentence variation from judge to judge and district to district. For each crime, a score was created. Particular characteristics of a crime could then add points: for instance, was a gun used? Was there a breach of public trust? Was the victim a minor? Furthermore, under the Guidelines, each defendant is given a criminal history score in an attempt to quantify his criminal propensity. The criminal history score is complex and may not tally crimes that occur before a particular date and may group certain crimes together if they are considered to be part of a common scheme. A grid then cross-references the crime score with the criminal history and informs the judge of the recommended potential sentencing range. The Guidelines are not currently mandatory (though they were for a period of time), but the Supreme Court requires that a federal judge refer to them and articulate the reasons for varying from the recommended range.

Creating the Guidelines was a colossal and enormously controversial effort. In 1984, Congress created the US Sentencing Commission to undertake the task as part of the Sentencing Reform Act. The Commission, which still exists, may consist of up to seven members serving six-year terms, all of whom are presidential appointees subject to Senate Confirmation. At its inception, the Commission collected data from 10,000 presentence investigations of defendants across the country. Then, through an elaborate and sometimes-opaque process, they selected numeric scores — each of which reflects a slew of theories of criminal justice. The AI risk assessment are merely the next steps in an ongoing process designed to bring evidence into risk assessment.

Accuracy of Human Risk Assessment: Pre-Trial Determinations

When I was a judge, I was constantly assessing risk in the decisions I made about pre-trial release, in the structure and duration of a sentence, and in what services might decrease the likelihood of recidivism. I am certain I was not right all the time, in part because I saw plenty of examples where my predictions ended up being wrong. With some frequency, I assessed that a defendant was unlikely to engage in criminal behavior prior to trial and released him on bail, only to be proven wrong when he was brought back to court having violated his bail terms. Often I was wrong in my initial judgment because I was convinced by the words and demeanor of the defendant. I believed him when he told me that he was on a different path, that he had structures in place that would keep temptation or opportunity at bay, or that it would be just plain stupid to commit any crimes before trial.

Drug addiction posed particularly difficult risk assessment problems. When a defendant was presented after a drug-related arrest and it was clear that he may have been motivated in part by a personal struggle with addiction, I often had to assess whether he would benefit more from being sent immediately to a drug program than jail. I sent many dozens of defendants to inpatient and outpatient drug programs in lieu of pre-trial detention. Often the defendants did well, and that success ultimately factored into their sentence. But occasionally, my assessment of the risk was wrong. Some defendants sold drugs while at the inpatient program; others sold drugs on the street outside an outpatient program, recruited gang members to commit violence on their behalf while in a program, or continued to engage in large scale drug distribution schemes while working full time in a completely lawful occupation.

My erroneous risk assessments were not limited to defendants arrested for drug crimes. In one instance, a young man arrested for fraud used his pre-trial freedom to continue various fraudulent schemes that resulted in hardworking people losing the money they needed to pay their rent or hold onto their homes. Another man arrested for a bank robbery sold stolen goods while on pre-trial release.

I considered myself a careful judge. I was certainly not a push over, and defendants who had been arrested for serious crimes did not enter my courtroom assuming they would have an easy time arranging release through bail terms. But I called it wrong a number of times. And, When I did so, I exposed the community to additional criminal conduct.

Accuracy of Human Risk Assessment: Sentencing

My experience as a judge at sentencing was similar. In instances in which there was no required mandatory minimum, I was able to exercise my discretion in imposing a sentence between "time served" and the upper end of whatever the criminal statute provided, informed by the Sentencing Guidelines. My analysis as to an appropriate sentence was based on a variety of factors including (1) the seriousness of the offense; (2) the nature and circumstances of the offense; and (3) the character of the defendant, including any potentially concerning or mitigating factors.

A judge has several tools at his disposal at sentencing. First, every criminal defendant in a federal case is entitled to a "presentence investigation report" (PSR). The PSR is based on information that the probation officer receives relating to the crime, the defendant's involvement, how the defendant has adjusted to prison if he was remanded pre-trial, and a host of personal information including educational, financial, and family background, along with any substance issues. A key portion of the PSR is a recitation of facts regarding any prior criminal conduct by the defendant.

Next, judges receive submissions from the defendant, often including letters from the defendant himself, family, friends, and colleagues. Judges also frequently receive a submission from the Government indicating its view of the crime and the role of the defendant. Plea agreements typically limit what both the defendant and the Government can argue about the duration of the sentence.

At the sentencing itself, the defendant is entitled to make a statement to the court regarding factors that might impact his sentence. During my time on the bench, a defendant's statement tended to include an apology to the United States, the courts, and the prosecutors, and then a discussion of how he would never again engage in criminal conduct. Since every defendant told me they would never commit another crime and yet frequently proceeded to do so, I separated these statements into three categories: (1) those made by a defendant who knew he was lying when he was saying it; (2) those made by a defendant who may have believed for a short period of time that he was committed to living a law-abiding life, but whose commitment was not strong enough to carry him through; and (3) those made by a defendant who was making a heartfelt and enduring commitment. It was my job to distinguish at least between the third category and the others, so that I could give credit to a person who had sincerely taken steps to change his life and avoid criminal conduct.

My judgment at sentencing was based in part on my assessment of whether a defendant needed to serve time as a retributive matter. This meant that the crime was serious enough that jail time was appropriate, whether or not he would ever reoffend; crimes of violence sometimes fit this category. But my sentence was also based on my personal assessment of the individual's character and likelihood of recidivating, and the extent to which any recidivism would harm the community or those around him.

My sentences, in other words, required prediction of risk. At the time of sentencing, there was no way for me to know whether my judgment about a particular defendant was correct or incorrect. When I was a new judge and had little experience, this was a particularly acute issue; I had as yet no experience with instances in which I was proven wrong and at least then developed some data to use in future proceedings.

But even today, several years after my last sentencing, for many individuals I do not know and will never know if my prediction was accurate. Many defendants who I judged as risks to the community are still in jail today. Others may have gotten out — but if they have committed a subsequent offense, it could easily be because prison tends to make people more prone to criminality rather than less so. In other words, I may have created a problem that had not previously existed. My experience as a judge in this regard is not unusual. Some judges may have a particular talent for assessing the person in front of them; other judges do not purport to have more than their personal judgment mixed with a lot of on-the-job experience.

In what percentage of cases were my risk assessments — done without the benefit of an AI risk assessment tool — accurate? I have no statistics. I have no idea how many of those I remanded — and who never had a chance to prove me wrong — would have in fact been crime free while awaiting trial. Nor do I have information that would allow me to better understand whether the sentences I imposed, based on a judgment about whether a defendant was likely to recidivate within a particular period of time, were right or wrong. Did I get it right 70% of the time? I hope I achieved better, but I don't know. Was I right 95% of the time? Even I doubt that could be the case — and based upon the breaks that I gave defendants and who proved my judgment ill-founded, I think there is likely enough data to know that 95% accuracy would be too high a number.

Comparing Human and AI Risk Assessment

As we move into our discussion of AI enabled risk assessment tools, it is reasonable to ask how we should be evaluating predictive accuracy. Is it reasonable and appropriate to compare accuracy of the tool to the accuracy of a human making similar decisions? Or do we expect more of the tools? Perhaps, if we are going to utilize tools to assist us, it is our expectation that the rate of accuracy will exceed that of an average human.

One complexity in answering questions relating to appropriate predictive accuracy is how little information we have regarding human accuracy. Current risk assessment tools are validated — that is, tested for accuracy. There are validation studies that occur before the release of a tool, but that validation is not done as a comparison to how accurate a human was or was not in his judgments, but as to whether the tool can accurately assess outcomes in a data set of static information.

Such tests do not exist for judges. It would be possible to design a study (and some have been done) that examines whether defendants released on bail commit crimes within a particular period of time. But it cannot be assumed from these studies that a judge was necessarily assessing risk of recidivism as anything other than what happened: it is certainly true that some judges know that a defendant is likely to commit a crime pre-trial, but deem the crime to be less harmful to the community as a whole than pre-trial detention. Similarly, some judges may assess a defendant at sentencing as likely to recidivate sooner rather than later but also deem the harm of incarceration to exceed the harm of the predicted crime.

We know, then, that as we approach risk assessment tools we should not be expecting 100% predictive accuracy; we also know that we will not really be able to determine how much better machines are as judges than humans. As we review existing AI-enabled risk assessment tools, we will see levels of accuracy in the ranges of 65–70%. We have to always remember that all of these predictions are based on aggregate analyses and not on an individual outcome.

In my view, we must insist on a base level of accuracy that meets or exceeds the average accuracy rate of a human performing the same task. Anything less makes the software worse than useless: it makes it unfair and harmful. We cannot give up on some form of normative testing and standard setting. Normative testing must include (as some validation tests do today) tests of tools against actual results.[2] It will take some time; a longitudinal study is needed. But we know that it is worth it in order to form an evidence-based view as to whether any tool, or one particular tool, is better at making these judgments than a human. To do so, we would need to understand how a judge assesses the risk profile of a particular individual, using the same criteria that a risk assessment tool uses. A normative test program can be performed for not just a single judge, or a single pre-trial officer, but for everyone: we allow the human to make a risk assessment, checking the boxes and explaining rationale according to the input factors in a hypothetical AI tool. It would also be important for the judicial officer to explain his rationale for a particular decision. The accuracy of these human decisions would be measured over a defined time period. Then, we would see what really happens: is the human risk assessment woefully inaccurate, a good predictor, or an excellent predictor? A comprehensive study of this kind would quiet a number of questions regarding fairness in our criminal justice system — but not all of them.

---

2 A controversial 2016 study by Angwin, Larson, Mattu, and Kirchner, did just that: they used a large sample of actual cases and compared them to predictions made by a particular tool (COMPAS). The results, the responses to which we will discuss, showed serious errors in the tool.

Chapter 7
AI Risk Assessment Tools: Achieving Moderate Accuracy

⚖️

We have now established that neither humans nor AI risk assessment tools can perfectly predict human behavior. But AI tools designed to assess risk, regardless of total accuracy, are at least consistent in outcome. That is, while humans may have all of the variability we have discussed in prior chapters, an AI tool designed in a particular way and provided with a particular set of facts ought to consistently provide the same answer. Daily events that might impact the human do not impact the machine. The tools, whatever their output, limit variability. But that lack of variability does not necessarily lead to results that are more "fair."

Accuracy versus Fairness

Accuracy does not, in and of itself, equate to fairness. Accuracy is whether a given prediction is correct. Fairness, on the other hand, requires an assessment of whether the applicable process is biased or not. Due process, as guaranteed by the US Constitution, is a guarantee of a fair process, and a fair process is associated with the most just result. As we will see in Chapter 10, design and data set limitations result in a widespread acceptance that AI risk assessment tools prioritize accuracy over fairness.

But just how accurate are these tools? Studies suggest they achieve accuracy rates of no more than between 60% and 70%.[1] The methodology to predict

---

1 See A. W. Flores, K. Bechtel, and C. T. Lowenkamp, "False Positives, False Negatives, and False Analyses: A Rejoinder to 'Machine Bias: There's Software Used Across the Country to Predict Future Criminals. And It's Biased Against Blacks," *Federal Probation Journal* 80(2) (2016), 41;

accuracy in this area is called "area under the curve" or "AUC"; the nuances of AUC are not critical to my argument, but some statisticians would debate whether "accuracy" and AUC perfectly correlate. As Skeem and Lowenkamp note in their study, AUCs are "widely used to assess the predictive utility of risk assessment instruments because it is readily interpretable;"[2] and, from Jackson and Mendoza: an AUC "represents the true discriminative ability of the scales."[3] According to the COMPAS guide itself, AUCs are the most "widely used measure of discrimination ability in criminal justice, psychology, medicine and related fields."[4] For the purposes of this book, the critical fact is that in the risk assessment area, accuracy and AUC are used as proxies for one another.

It bears noting that the 60–70% accuracy rate obscures a more startling unfairness: the tools are materially worse at predicting recidivism and violence for Black defendants than for white ones. This too must be measured against human error in relationship to race. I explore this race-specific issue in Chapter 10.

The most well-known risk assessment tool is COMPAS, made by Northpointe (d/b/a Equivant). Northpointe publishes and periodically updates a Practitioner's Guide to the COMPAS Core.[5] This Guide states that risk assessment tools are better than human decision-making, and references two oft-cited articles: Grove, Zald, Lebow, Snitz and Nelson ("Grove"), and Swets, Dawes and Monahan ("Swets"). These same studies are cited in connection

---

J. L. Skeem and C. Lowenkamp, "Risk, Race & Recidivism: Predictive Bias and Disparate Impact," (2016), p. 12. Available at SSRN: https://ssrn.com/abstract=2687339 or http://dx.doi.org/10.2139/ssrn.2687339; J. Dressel and H. Farid, "The Accuracy, Fairness and Limits of Predicting Recidivism," Science Advances 4(1), (2018), 2, DOI: 10.1126/sciadv.aao5580; E. Jackson and C. Mendoza, "Setting the Record Straight: What the COMPAS Core Risk and Need Assessment is and is Not," *Harvard Data Science Review* 2(1) (2020), 7; J. Skeem and C. T. Lowenkamp, "Using Algorithms to Address Trade-Offs Inherent in Predicting Recidivism," *Behavioral Sciences & the Law* 38(1) (2020), DOI: 10.1002/bsl.2465.

2   J. Skeem and C. T. Lowenkamp, "Using Algorithms to Address Trade-Offs Inherent in Predicting Recidivism," *Behavioral Sciences & the Law* 38(1) (2020), DOI: 10.1002/bsl.2465.

3   E. Jackson and C. Mendoza, "Setting the Record Straight: What the COMPAS Core Risk and Need Assessment is and is Not," *Harvard Data Science Review* 2(1) (2020), p. 6

4   COMPAS Practitioner's Guide (2020, p. 13).

5   Guide (2019).

with the federal Post Conviction Risk Assessment (PCRA) tool as a basis for choosing imperfect tools over human decision-making.[6]

But neither the Grove nor the Swets article provide a solid basis for choosing machine over man. First, neither article studies *AI* risk assessment tools. Instead, both articles broadly explore the use of actuarial and statistical methods to assess the accuracy of clinical judgments in a wide variety of areas — medical, educational, and business, to name a few. Each article concludes that human clinical judgment is more prone to inaccuracy than when actuarial data is used to make a specific statement.

Criminal recidivism is mentioned only a handful of times. Grove — referred to as a "meta-analysis" because it does not itself present a new study but instead analyzes other, published studies — reviews the outcomes of over 100 studies published between 1936 and 1989. Of those, only nine assessed recidivism, assaultive behavior, or parole success or failure. For each of the nine, the results showed relatively insignificant differences for all but one.[7] The one study that did have a truly notable difference in accuracy between human clinical judgment and actuarial studies was a 1988 study by G.C.N. Hall. Hall's study, "Criminal Behavior as a Function of Clinical and Actuarial Variables in a Sexual Offender Population," examined actuarial variables relating to adult sexual offenses, and found that for the population studied, clinical judgment was not significantly predictive. The *most* significant results from the Grove article show that mechanical assessments exceed clinical predictions in the areas of college academic performance, the rate of throat infection, the diagnosis of gastrointestinal disorders, and abdominal pain.

The Swets article also has a number of shortcomings when relied on in the AI assessment tool context. It does not purport to measure accuracy itself, but instead posits a methodology for improving diagnostic decision-making

---

6   Grove, Zald, Lebow, Snitz, and Nelson, "Clinical Versus Mechanical Prediction: A Meta-Analysis," (2000), *Psychological Assessment* 12(1): 19–30. DOI: 10.1037/1040-3590.12.1.19, is cited in numerous papers for the superiority of machine over human decision-making. For the reasons discussed, strong reliance on this article is misplaced.

7   Grove (2000, pp. 22–24).

through the use of statistical analyses. Swet and his colleagues recognize that:

> *More complex computer-based systems have not done well.* It may well be that computer-based systems for two-alternative diagnoses suffer by inappropriate generalization from experience with medical systems built to contend with more complex diagnoses, in which the diagnostician describes a patient's symptoms and looks for a listing of diseases that should be discovered. Such systems have been based on artificial intelligence (expert systems), probabilistic reasoning, a combination of the two, or on other methods. Performance deficiencies of four prominent examples were reviewed by Berner *et al.* (1994). An accompanying editorial in the New England Journal of Medicine gave these examples a grade of "C".[8]

Swet further speculates: "It may well be that one particular hindrance just mentioned is sufficient to preclude use of a [statistical prediction rule] or of an analysis of decision utility in a given situation."[9]

In 2015, the National Center for State Courts published a series of "observations" drawn from ten jurisdictions that used risk assessment tools in connection with sentencing.[10] This report doubles down on the assertion that AI tools are more accurate in their predictions with carefully reassuring anecdotes. It references defense counsel who indicated that the tool was "helpful," and that they believed "that the use of RNA information has resulted in more consistent and objective sentencing decisions."[11] The report also highlights observations from judges: "One judge noted, for example, that RNA information provides a basis for more rational, and less subjective, decision-making."[12] Another judge is quoted as saying:

> These risk/needs assessment tools give me a way of checking myself, that I'm not sentencing out of anger, that I'm not sentencing out of an inappropriate

---

8   Swets, Dawes, and Monahan, (2000, p. 22) (internal citation omitted).

9   *Ibid.*

10 J. K. Elek, R. K. Warren, and P. M. Casey, "Using Risk and Needs Assessment Information at Sentencing: Observations from Ten Jurisdictions", (National Center for State Courts, 2015).

11 *Ibid.*, p.t 31.

12 *Ibid.*, p. 32.

place, but that I have some objective criteria upon which to decide what to do with individuals' lives because it's a huge responsibility to make decisions about what we're going to do with a person's life. And how do we protect our public in doing that? So that's really been I think the biggest positive for me is it takes out that "I know better" paternal gut thing out of my equation.[13]

Frequently, defenses of the error rate of risk assessment tools versus human error rates feel like Russian nesting dolls: one study citing to another study, that cites to another study, and on. The 2017 Federal Probation Department study that examined racial bias (Flores, Bechtel, and Lowenkamp) ("Flores") in PCRA engages in this form of defense. The Flores report defends the PCRA error rate as at least better than human error rate with the blunt assertion that "[t]he issue that is no longer up for debate is that ARAIs [actuarial risk assessment instrument] predict outcomes more strongly and accurately than professional judgment alone."[14] It cites the same Grove article that COMPAS cites, as well as a 2009 meta-analysis ("Hanson") that also reviews prior academic literature.[15] The Hanson article itself refers to yet more articles in support of the proposition that "[i]t is widely accepted that evaluations based on unstructured professional judgment are less accurate than structured risk assessments."[16] Hanson then synthesizes and analyzes a variety of studies primarily from the United States, Canada, and the United Kingdom:

> The accumulated research record clearly shows that it is possible for clinicians to predict without understanding a particular individual and that the subjective feeling of "understanding" need not lead to accurate predictions about future behavior.[17]

---

13 *Ibid.*, p.t 33.

14 A. W. Flores, K. Bechtel, and C. T. Lowenkamp, "False Positives, False Negatives, and False Analyses: A Rejoinder to 'Machine Bias: There's Software Used Across the Country to Predict Future Criminals. And it's Biased Against Blacks", *Federal Probation,* 80(2) (2016), 39.

15 *Ibid.* (citing R. K. K. Hanson and K. E. Morton-Bourgon, "The Accuracy of Recidivism Risk Assessments for Sexual Offenders: A Meta-Analysis of 118 Prediction Studies", *Psychological Assessment* 21(1) (2009), 1–21, DOI: 10.1037/a0014421).

16 citing Andrews, Bonta, Wormith, (2006); Janus and Prentky, (2003); Monahan, (2007); Quinsey, Harris, Rice and Cormier, (2006).

17 Quinsey *et al.* (2006, p. 2).

Studies convincing the reader that tools are better than humans at predicting human behavior may comfort licensors and users, but they likely provide little reassurance to individuals whose liberty is at risk. One of the creators of a widely used tool, the LSI-R (now the LS/CMI), James Bonta, acknowledges that the purposes of risk assessment tools can be as much about justification as about assessment:

> Risk assessment is a double-edged sword. It can be used to justify the application of severe sanctions or to moderate extreme penalties. It is easy to "sell" a risk instrument when the instrument claims to identify the dangerous and justifies the imprisonment of those individuals ... And considering the high levels of incarceration, I sometimes wonder whether risk instruments serve to identify the highly dangerous a priori or simply serve to justify decisions already made.[18]

Bonta, who repeatedly expresses his view that punishment of offenders should use the least intrusive measures, also provided the following revealing anecdote:

> Larry Motiuk, who worked with me on a number of these projects, joked that maybe the name [of the LSI-R tool] should be changed from Level of Service Inventory to "Locked Securely Inside."[19]

A compelling study by Dressel and Farid sought to predict recidivism and, in particular, racial skew by directly testing the relative accuracy between AI tools and human decision-making. With regard to accuracy of predictions, it found little to no difference between the two, but it also demonstrated that the machine's reliance on historical data yielded racially disparate results.[20]

Specifically, the study was a stylized comparison of the COMPAS tool to decisions made by humans that were solicited from an Internet survey site. The

---

18 J. Bonta, "Offender Risk Assessment: Guidelines for Selection and Use", (2002), p. 375, https://doi.org/10.1177/0093854802029004002.

19 *Ibid.*

20 J. Dressel and H. Farid, "The Accuracy, Fairness, and Limits of Predicting Recidivism," *Science Advances* 4(1) (2018), eaao5580, DOI: 10.1126/sciadv.aao5580.

purpose was to "compare the overall accuracy and bias in human assessment with the algorithmic assessment in COMPAS."[21] The study sought to measure "overall accuracy as the rate at which the defendant is correctly predicted to recidivate or not (that is, true-positive and true-negative rates)."[22]

A total of 1000 defendant descriptions were used.[23] Participants were given short fictional case synopses including the age, sex, and previous criminal history of the defendant, but were not told his race.[24] They were then asked to predict whether this person was likely to recidivate within 2 years.[25] The human accuracy for Black defendants was 68.2%, compared with 67.6% accuracy for white ones. The human false positive rate for Black defendants was 37.1%, compared with 27.2% for white. The human false negative rate for Black defendants was 29.2%, compared to 40.4% for white.[26]

The AUC measure of predictive accuracy, for both the humans and the COMPAS tool, were nearly identical: human participants had an AUC of their pooled results of 0.71, while the AUC for COMPAS was 0.70.[27] The predictive accuracy for black defendants was 68.2% versus 67.6% for white (again, nearly identical).[28] The authors of the study concluded that humans "who, it can reasonably be assumed, have little to no expertise in criminal justice — are as accurate and fair as COMPAS in predicting recidivism."[29]

---

21 *Ibid.*, p. 1.

22 *Ibid.*

23 *Ibid.*, p. 2.

24 *Ibid.*

25 *Ibid.*

26 *Ibid.*

27 *Ibid.*, p. 3.

28 *Ibid.*

29 *Ibid.*

In sum, it is far from a foregone conclusion that AI risk assessment tools are more accurate than human decision-makers, particularly in the area of criminal justice. What *is* known is that these tools have *in*accuracy rates that sometimes exceed 30%. These studies are weak and insufficient to prove accuracy in most contexts, but are particularly unacceptable as "proof" in the context of liberty decisions.

Chapter 8
COMPAS: Case Study of an AI Risk Assessment Tool

⚖️

The best-studied and most widely-utilized AI assessment tool now on the market is COMPAS.[1] COMPAS's designers publish a guide ("Guide") containing a variety of information about how the tool works, and how it should be interpreted and used.[2] The Guide does not disclose what machine learning method it is based on, or its algorithm, precise inputs, weightings, or data sets used.[3]

The Guide is explicitly a theoretically-driven model, based on designer-selection of normative theories for criminal conduct. These theoretical choices heavily influence which inputs the designers chose and how they chose to weigh them. It reveals that the tool is based on factors drawn from academic research, some of which is cited in the Guide. The Guide also explicitly acknowledges that its

---

1 COMPAS is made by Northpointe (d/b/a Equivant), originally founded by Timothy Brennan. Brennan remains the Chief Scientist for Northpointe, though the company has been sold. One of his areas of expertise is machine learning — and ahe has written generally on the use of machine learning in connection with risk assessment tools. T. Brennan and W. L. Oliver, "The Emergence of Machine Learning Techniques in Criminology," *Criminology & Public Policy*, 12(3) (2013).

2 Practitioner's Guide to COMPAS Core (2020) (www.equivant/resources).

3 It may be that COMPAS chose to both signal and then downplay the tool's reliance on machine learning for precisely the concerns about public reaction that Brennan flagged in his 2013 article discussed in Chapter Two. The COMPAS Guide states only that "[t]here are different statistical approaches to predictive modeling. Machine learning methods are highly flexible and are usually preferred in applications where there is a complex relationship between predictors and outcomes." Guide, p. 13; citing R Berk, *Criminal Justice Forecasts of Risk: A Machine Learning Approach.* Springer Publishing Company, 2012, and R. Berk and J. Bleich, "Statistical Procedures for Forecasting Criminal Behavior: A Comparative Assessment", *American Society of Criminology, Criminology & Public Policy*, 12(3), (2013). The Guide continues, "[t]he methods used to develop both risk scales are described in various books on regression modeling and machine learning" (Guide, p. 13).

results are impacted by structural inequalities over which an offender has no control, and, notably, states that it does not make compensating adjustments.[4]

The inputs used in the COMPAS tool design reveal a number of clear embedded biases. I am not suggesting that any bias is intentional or malicious, but rather that it does exist in this and other tools being used to make liberty decisions. My exploration of the COMPAS tool begins with its name, then reviews the research used to develop the tool, and finally turns to how COMPAS has been tested for accuracy and how it has been criticized.

COMPAS: What's in a Name?

COMPAS stands for "Correctional Offender Management Profiling for Alternative Sanctions." The name alone sets the stage for a discussion about embedded biases. Let's break it down, phrase by phrase.

"Correctional Offender" appears to be a straight-forward factual statement locating this tool's primary usage. But the term "correctional" instantly conjures law enforcement: a house of correction, a department of correction, correction management, and so forth. The term is thus inflected with a law-enforcement perspective from the outset. Moreover, it conveys a normative ethical view that the "offender" can be "corrected" or changed.

"Management" refers both to management of the offender — that is how the human who is being assessed will be managed — and how the process of assessment will be managed. Management, in this context, can be seen as a form of control. Meanwhile "Profiling" is revealing and descriptive: the tool is directed at taking statistical information and creating profiles of offenders, and then distributing the offenders among various risk categories. Profiles are not in-depth psychological studies, nor are they detailed analyses of how a specific individual will, would, or could act in a specific situation. Rather, profiles based on aggregate statistics are generalizations, which run the risk of conforming to perceived stereotypes. As a result, the concept of "profiling" is strongly disfavored by many people on all sides of criminal justice issues.

---

4   Guide, p. 19.

The final phrase — "Alternative Solutions" — provides a hopeful suggestion that the tool has been created to assist with an unspecified substitute for incarceration. Northpointe confirms this potential use, writing in the Guide that COMPAS can assist with identifying programs and services that a particular defendant may need in order to limit or eliminate the risk of recidivism.[5]

In sum, what do we learn from the COMPAS name? We learn that it is a tool with a tenable connection to law enforcement, and that it uses profiling as its primary management technique. We also learn that it holds out the potential for rehabilitative solutions beyond or in addition to incarceration.

The Guide

The COMPAS Practitioner's Guide is a 68-page document providing some explanation (though far from a complete one) as to how the COMPAS tool was created, how it has been validated, and how it should be interpreted.[6] At least one state supreme court has cited an earlier version of the Guide as providing sufficient transparency to a defendant to avoid a due process violation.[7]

The Guide is an extraordinary document: a goldmine of information not only about this particular instrument, but about how similar instruments are likely constructed. At the outset, it defines the purpose of COMPAS: to provide an analysis of "predictors that affect recidivism."[8] The COMPAS designers have selected which predictors to evaluate and then determined which ones are most likely to affect recidivism.

Notably, there is no transparency as to the educational or professional background of the COMPAS personnel involved in the tool's design. We do

---

5   Guide, p. 51.

6   As discussed in several places, much about the machine learning method and underlying algorithmic structure of the COMPAS tool remains unknown. An interesting article on the lack of transparency of the tool was published by C. Rudin, C. Wang, and B. Coker, "The Age of Secrecy and Unfairness in Recidivism Prediction", *HDSR* (2020).

7   *Loomis v. Wisconsin*, 881 N.W.2d 749 (Wis. 2016), cert. denied, 137 S. Ct. 2290 (2017).

8   Guide, p. 1.

know some information about Northpointe's founder, Tim Brennan, who has a Ph.D. from Lancaster University and is identified as a criminologist.[9] He is also a regular lecturer for the National Institute of Corrections. But this general lack of detail is important because, for factor selection, weighting, and interpretation, COMPAS is reliant on theoretical choices by its design team. As the Guide tells the reader: "Each COMPAS scale [there are both risk and needs scales] has been constructed based on a variety of behavioral and psychological constructs that are of very high relevance to recidivism and criminal careers" and "research/literature supports the scale content and context."[10]

The Guide acknowledges that it has taken into account unspecified tradeoffs in the COMPAS tool between "comprehensive coverage of key risk and criminogenic factors" and "brevity and practicality."[11] It deals with that trade off by "provid[ing] a comprehensive set of key risk factors that have emerged from recent criminological literature, and ... allow[ing] for customization inside the software."[12] The term "customization" makes clear that human selection is involved in determining algorithmic design — the inputs and possibly the weightings. The word choice also confirms that COMPAS personnel have used "criminological literature" as a basis for algorithmic design choices: "[The COMPAS tool] provides a comprehensive set of key risk factors that have *emerged* from the recent criminological literature."[13] The reference to using criminological literature is significant, as it dispels any notion that AI-enabled risk assessments are based solely on what the machine learning tools identify as patterns in a data set. In other words, humans really are involved in determining the methology of the tool.

---

9   www.linkedin.com/tim-brennan-b0313ab; equivant.com/browsebyblog/AI-and-human-decision-making-brennan.

10 Guide, p. 30.

11 *Ibid.*, p. 2.

12 *Ibid.*

13 *Ibid.*, p. 2, emphasis added.

Criminological Theories

Though it does not state how it chose among competing theories or whether it has engaged critically with them, the Guide provides a fairly detailed description of the "criminological theories used in COMPAS."[14] While several of the broad categories are widely accepted in criminological literature, several are more controversial.

One category that the Guide refers to is the "Social Learning Theory." The stated principle of this theory is that behavior is modeled, imitated, and if reinforced then likely to recur again."[15] Embedded in Social Learning Theory, as evidenced by the social science research which it cites, are concepts such as parental or close adult criminal behavior translating into modeled behavior for a particular individual. The use of this theory in design choice therefore has immediate implications for communities in which parents are more likely to have been arrested or incarcerated.

An even more controversial theory is the one referred to as the "Sub-Culture Theory."[16] The Sub-Culture theory, which was developed from literature about the "Chicago School on Gangs," suggests that norms are transmitted through social interactions, that norms in sub-cultures differ from those in the main culture, and that certain behaviors become a cultural norm within the sub-culture. The Guide explains that this theory — to which COMPAS ascribes — is based on a view that "[a]ll individuals in society are driven toward economic success. Some subcultures aim to achieve that success through illegitimate means."[17]

A third criminological theory that the Guide references is the "Control/Restraint Theory." This theory posits that criminal tendencies may develop if an individual

---

14 *Ibid.*, p. 3.

15 *Ibid.*, p. 5.

16 *Ibid.*, p. 5.

17 *Ibid.*

is "bonded" to antisocial norms, values and associations, and his level of status depends on adherence to the restraints of that norm group.[18]

Two final theories worth a mention are the "Criminal Opportunity (including Routine Activity)" and the "Social Strain" theories. The former relates to economic motivations.[19] The latter theory is sometimes referred to as the "'means-end' theory of deviance."[20] It is based on a view that "[c]rime breeds in the gap between culturally induced aspirations and structurally distributed possibilities for success."[21] In other words, if you are born into a community in which everyone has more than you do, and you want what they have, but your personal opportunities are limited, you may experience social strain that leads to criminal conduct. The Guide further describes this theory as "the combination of cultural emphasis and social structure which produce intense pressure for deviation-criminal behavior."[22] Finally, the Guide tells us that the designers view "[c]rime [as] occurr[ing] largely in poverty-stricken areas where opportunities to attain the 'American Dream' by legitimate means [are] blocked, producing frustration and a desire to pursue monetary success by any means necessary."[23]

Even with a cursory review of these theories, potential problems rise to the surface. While theories like "Social Strain" and "Sub-Culture" are supposed to be objective — or at least factually-based — criminological views, it is easy to see how quickly a Black, Brown, or low-income individual can get swept into a theoretical presumption of criminality. Without a more transparent understanding of how and why these theories were chosen to underly COMPAS (and even that might not be enough), it is difficult to see how the tool itself can be objective in its determinations of risk. As the saying goes: a poisoned tree cannot bear good fruit.

---

18 *Ibid.*, p. 5–6.

19 *Ibid.*, p. 6.

20 *Ibid.*

21 *Ibid.*

22 *Ibid.*

23 *Ibid.*

Needs Scales

The Guide also outlines a set of "needs scales" based on its normative views.[24] These scales are designed to assist court systems with planning services that might deter a defendant from further criminal conduct. The needs scales also, however, synthesize data to present a profile of the offender that is used by judicial officers in connection with their overall assessment. Normative judgments can therefore be transmitted to decision-makers as a portrait of who this offender is.

Among the key needs predictors is whether the offender has "criminal associates/peers."[25] This category allows COMPAS to perceive "involvement with anti-social friends and associates" as a significant risk factor for criminality."[26] In addition, designers chose "affiliating with aggressive and criminal others" as a significant risk factor for "further violence and crime."[27] The Guide states that "[t]his is consistent with both social learning theory and sub-cultural theories of crime."[28]

Another needs scale relates to "[c]riminal involvement."[29] The Guide states: "This scale is defined by the extent of the person's involvement in the criminal justice system. A high score indicates a person who has multiple arrests, multiple convictions and prior incarcerations."[30] The scale is designed to utilize "arrest history" in determining behavioral patterns for the defendant: "Arrest history is useful here to see patterns (persons, places, things, times of year) and other related elements that could be antecedents to recidivism and perhaps causal factors (thoughts, feelings, beliefs and attitudes) that can be impacted by intervention."[31]

---

24 *Ibid.*, p. 36.

25 *Ibid.*

26 *Ibid.*

27 *Ibid.*, p. 37.

28 *Ibid.*, p. 30.

29 *Ibid.*, p. 37.

30 *Ibid.*

31 *Ibid.*, p. 38.

The Guide then lists "criminal opportunity," which "emerges from criminological theories that stress the importance of routine daily activities and the importance of occupying certain social roles (marriage, parenting, being an employee). These roles tend to structure a person's daily activities in a pro-social manner."[32] Information about a defendant's early life also plays a role in defining where he falls on the scale.[33] The central items undergirding this theory are "being unemployed, living in a high crime area, having friends who engage in drug use, and having no constructive activities."[34]

COMPAS's additional needs scales are designed around concepts of "criminal personality," "criminal thinking," "family criminality," and "financial problems."[35] With regard to family criminality, the Guide states:

> Research has consistently demonstrated that delinquency and adult crime are both associated with parent criminality. (West, 1973; Lyken, 1995). Children may learn that violent and deviant behavior "work" in the context of their family. Aside from the social learning and role modeling perspective, other intergenerational mechanisms may operate to transmit values and behaviors from parent to child. Genetic influences, for example, may operate to transmit anti-social personality disorder and criminality. (Lykken, 1995). COMPAS therefore includes a measure of family criminality focusing on the criminality and drug use history of the mother, father and siblings."[36]

COMPAS refers to the "financial problems" risk factor as "linked to lower social class, poor housing, community disorganization and other factors."[37] The model uses "[a]imlessness in the use of leisure time," and "residential instability" as additional risk factors for criminal behavior.[38]

---

32 *Ibid.*

33 *Ibid.*

34 *Ibid.*

35 *Ibid.*, pp. 39–42.

36 *Ibid.*, p. 42. (internal citations omitted)

37 *Ibid.*

38 *Ibid.*, pp.t 44–45.

The Guide also refers to the general category of "social environment" as presenting risk of recidivism:

> Living in a high crime neighborhood is a well-established correlate of both delinquency and adult crime. (Thornberry, Huizanga & Loeber, 1995; Sampson & Lauritsen, 1994). This risk factor fits into several theoretical models of crime and delinquency (e.g., social disorganization, social learning, and sub-cultural theories). Disorganized and high crime communities are characterized by perceived high crime rates, gangs, easy access to drugs, and inadequate housing.[39]

According to the Guide, "[t]his scale focuses on the amount of crime, disorder, and victimization potential in the neighborhood in which a person lives."[40]

The Guide further discusses "Socialization failure" as a risk factor:

> We have constructed a higher order factor in COMPAS that builds on the early onset of delinquency, problem behavior in school (dropout, suspensions, fighting, etc.), inadequate parental socialization, and early drug use. These are all well-known risk factors for later criminality (Chaiken, Chaiken, & Rhodes, 1994; Lykken, 1995) and all represent early socialization problems.[41]

Altogether, it is clear that these "risk factors" are consistent with structural associations of criminality — and it is precisely these structural associations that cloud the objectivity of COMPAS. For example, if you were born and raised in a public housing project with a high crime rate, you immediately accumulate a number of risk factors in your needs assessment. If you dropped out of your local public high school in the eleventh grade — perhaps because the school was wildly underfunded and you felt that you were better off entering the workforce — that is another knock on your risk factor. And, of course, the common thread in these hypothetical circumstances is race (and, to an extent, class): Black and Brown people are much more likely than white

---

39 *Ibid.*, p.t 46.

40 *Ibid.*

41 *Ibid.*, p. 47.

people to live in public housing and attend underfunded public schools; this is well known. In fact, almost every risk factor stated in the needs scales section of the Guide could be a code word for race: prior incarcerations, arrest history, living in a high crime area, poor parental role models, gang and drug activity. So, in reality, the needs predictors — which help determine a judge's assessment of a defendant — cannot be divorced from structural, societal stereotypes about race, class, and crime. In this way, once COMPAS gets involved, it becomes even more difficult to break this presumption of criminality.

COMPAS Typologies

The COMPAS tool separates offenders into "typologies" using a form of machine learning pattern recognition.[42] That is, based on a variety of information, some of which is drawn from a questionnaire that the offender fills out (or is filled out by a probation or pre-trial officer interviewing the offender), he is placed into a "typology." The typology is a significant profiling exercise, designed to describe who an offender is for purposes of informing his case plan. As COMPAS describes it:

> Each person is now automatically classified on the basis of the "best fit" to one of several standard and replicated needs profiles. The class profile of each person is automatically produced as part of the standard report to help treatment staff conceptualize the "kind" of client they are dealing with.[43]

COMPAS therefore determines the offender's "identity using advanced, unknown statistical methods that "suggest a beginning 'framework' for a case plan."[44] The case plan may have significant liberty implications. It can be determinative as to the selection of the amount of supervision to which a defendant is subject as well

---

42 *Ibid.*, p. 51 ("These typologies use a form of advanced pattern recognition, cross-validation procedures and multiple methods to verify the stability of the typologies.")

43 *Ibid.*

44 *Ibid.*

as potential programmatic and treatment options.[45] The typologies are also gendered, with eight distinct options for men and eight distinct options for women.

The male typologies are:

Cat. 1: Chronic drug abusers — most non-violent

Cat. 2: Low risk/situational — fighting/domestic violence caution

Cat. 3: Chronic alcohol problems — DUI, domestic violence

Cat. 4: Socially marginalized — poor, uneducated, stressed, habitual offenders

Cat. 5: Criminally versatile — young, marginalized persons often gang affiliated

Cat. 6: Socially isolated long-term substance abuse

Cat. 7: Serious versatile high-risk individuals

Cat. 8: Low risk situational accidental[46]

The female typologies are:

Cat. 1: Drug problems and anti-social sub-cultural influences — some with relationship conflicts

Cat. 2: Family disorganization and inadequate parenting — residential instability and minor non-violent offenses

Cat. 3: Chronic substance abusers — women with higher social resources than other groups

Cat. 4: Marginalized poor and isolated women — economic survival crimes

Cat. 5: Young, anti-social poorly educated women with some violent offenses and early delinquent onset

Cat. 6: Chronic long-term history A — multiple co-occurring social and psychological risk factors

Cat. 7: Chronic long-term history B — multiple co-occurring problems and high risk

Cat. 8: Late starters with multiple strengths and fewer risk factors — minor non-violent offense history[47]

---

45 *Ibid.*, p. 52.

46 *Ibid.*, pp. 54–58.

47 *Ibid.*, pp. 59–61.

These gendered typologies are likely created from the machine learning "random forest" techniques we discussed in Chapter 2, and are likely endorsed by COMPAS's designers.[48] But without adequate transparency into the model design, we cannot know for certain. What is clear, however, is that there is a lot embedded in these typologies about how a person can be categorized, and that this categorization is then used throughout the plan (including release and terms of supervision) developed for a person.

The COMPAS Data Set

The Guide contains only a single paragraph on the data set that the tool uses.[49] As we know from the discussion of how machine learning and other forms of AI algorithms work, the data set is central to all output.

The information contained within any given data set instructs an AI tool that certain characteristics and patterns are or are not relevant to an outcome. So, for instance, if all the data for an "offender data base" is for men under the age of 35, the tool will learn that being both male and under the age of 35 are highly correlated with criminality. If the data is drawn from a particular region that had policing policies in place that impacted the demographics of the arrestee or offender population, that plainly matters.[50]

The methodology behind the COMPAS data set is unclear. Between January 2004 and November 2005, COMPAS designers interviewed 30,000 people who had, to different extents, been brought into the criminal intake process. To rephrase: while some of these 30,000 interviewees were currently incarcerated, some had only been arrested and were awaiting next steps, and others had finished their sentences and were out on probation. This is all to say that this pool of 30,000 was by no means uniform. COMPAS designers

---

48 T. Brennan and W. L. Oliver, "The Emergence of Machine Learning Techniques in Criminology," *Criminology & Public Policy*, 12(3) (2013).

49 *Ibid.*, p. 11.

50 COMPAS states that "[c]ore norm data are evaluated through client norm studies. Agency-specific norm groups are developed for some clients" (Guide, p. 11). It is unclear what this means — and I do not read it to suggest, for instance, that data sets are specific to jurisdiction or any particular time period.

then whittled this group of 30,000 down to a norm group of 7,381 "offenders." Again, it is unclear why this group of 7,381 was chosen as the "norm" group; lack of transparency is, of course, a theme.

What we do know is that this data set is frozen in time. Even as COMPAS makes analyses of criminal defendants in 2020, it is using a data set from the early 2000s. This is problematic, to say the least, particularly given the lack of transparency in the initial compilation of the data. It is possible that judges in California are using COMPAS, which uses data from when marijuana arrests in the state were high among racial minorities, to make a current risk and needs assessment of a Black male defendant. This scenario sounds problematic, but it's also hypothetically possible that because of the way the data was gathered and assembled there is no extra risk to this defendant. The stark reality is that we just don't know — and we can't properly trust the assessments of COMPAS until we do.

The little we do know about the demographics of the data set may only increase our worry. The Guide does reveal that men represent 76.9% of the norm group while women represent 23.1%. Further, and more concerningly, the set reflects the over-representation of Black people in the American criminal justice system. While Black Americans comprised 13% of the population in 2005 — a proportion that has only increased to 13.4% in 2020 — they make up 24.9% of the data set. On the flipside, while Latinos make up 18% of the current population, they only represent 10.3% of the COMPAS norm group. Caucasians are also slightly underrepresented in the 2004–5 norm group: while they comprise just 61.6% of the norm population, they make up 63.4% of the 2020 United States population.

The Guide also does not break down the data by region. In fact, it appears that data for arrestees from different regions was combined. In other words, the designers of the tool don't seem to acknowledge that there might be variations in patterns of criminal behavior (or arrest) from region to region. A data set drawn from Philadelphia, Pennsylvania may provide inaccurate predictions for a defendant from South Dakota, or even for a defendant from the Pennsylvania state capital of Harrisburg — a much smaller city in a totally different part of the state.

A holistic consideration of the COMPAS data set therefore yields several implications. First, the Guide indicates that initial data set assessments were drawn from all stages of the criminal process: pre-trial through post-conviction. This means that the tool may predict patterns of recidivism based on data drawn, in part, from individuals who were never convicted of a crime. Second, the data set has apparently not been updated in almost two decades, which means that it does not reflect any recent decriminalization efforts or changing societal attitudes toward certain drugs. Perhaps, then, the data set provides an outdated picture of a typical criminal. Or, the data set may provide an over or underexaggerated picture of criminality: the overrepresentation of Black defendants and simultaneous underrepresentation of other races. And, finally, there is no known accounting for regional differences in crime, which is problematic for reasons previously discussed. On the whole, what we know about the COMPAS data set is that it reflects well-known structural inequalities and controversial policing practices (like Stop and Frisk, which was not officially ended until 2013), and it may not differentiate between region or pre versus post-trial status. This lack of transparency requires one to wonder what the tool can predict and for whom.

COMPAS and Predictive Accuracy

We have already described COMPAS's inputs, its algorithm and data sets. But what of its outputs? Risk assessment tools are tested — or "validated" — for predictive accuracy. One could argue that if predictive accuracy is sufficiently high, the specific issues in the data set, input selection, or weighting are less concerning. But no AI risk assessment tool achieves accuracy rates above 75% on a consistent basis, and the most widely-used tools hover in the 60–71% range.[51]

To measure accuracy, we look at the "AUC Score" — the "area under the curve." AUC scores are generally broken into scored categories of "poor," "fair," "good," and "excellent." COMPAS uses the following cut offs for each category: below

---

51 In a YouTube video of Tim Brennan, COMPAS's creator and chief scientist, released in the spring of 2020, he describes the machine learning for COMPAS as resulting in accuracy of between 60% and 70%. (https://www.youtube.com/watch?v=kOh0i3hpqNg)

0.65 is considered poor predictive accuracy, 0.65–0.69 is considered fair, 0.70–0.75 is considered good, and above 0.76 is excellent.[52]

The association of what constitutes "poor, fair, good, and excellent" must be understood as normative judgments. In the context of liberty decisions, a score that leaves open the possibility of a 24% rate of incorrect predictions can hardly be considered "excellent." An offender who falls victim to that 24% would be unlikely to perceive the tool as providing "excellent" reliability.

COMPAS has disclosed several validation studies performed between 2009 and 2018. The tool's AUC score ranges from 0.63 to 0.71 for violent offenders (the poor to good range) and 0.69–0.73 for non-violent offenders (fair to good).[53] COMPAS has also compared its AUC results to those for other, similar tools, and has found that they compare favorably.[54] According to the Guide, a 2017 study of a tool created specifically for Ohio (the "ORAS" tool), found AUCs only in the 0.60s.[55]

Some state entities have performed their own validation studies on the COMPAS tool. A 2012 validation study by New York State's Division of Criminal Justice Services found that "the Recidivism Scale worked effectively and achieved satisfactory predictive accuracy."[56] A 2016 study, also focused on New York State, examined its "mental health court" use of COMPAS. That study measured an AUC of 0.70 for general recidivism, and between 0.65 and 0.67 within specific risk categories.[57]

No published validation studies that I am aware of report AUC scores of 80%, let alone 90%. That kind of accuracy has not yet been achieved.

---

52 Guide, p. 13.

53 *Ibid.*, p. 16.

54 *Ibid.*, pp. 20–21.

55 *Ibid.*, p. 20.

56 S. Lansing, "New York State COMPAS-Probation Risk and Need Assessment Study," *The Division of Criminal Justice Services* (2012), Exec. Summary.

57 W. A. Reich, S. Picard-Fritshe, V. B. Rioja, and M. R. Rotter, "Evidence-Based Risk Assessment in a Mental Health Court" *Risk Assessment in Mental Health Court* (2016), Exec. Summary.

Predictive Accuracy and Race

One clear result of many validation studies is that predictive accuracy varies by race. In Chapter 10, I discuss the trade-off between accuracy and fairness in the context of liberty decisions. For now, the basic point is that validation studies have shown demonstrated racial disparities.

The COMPAS Guide both acknowledges the finding and denies the validity of these disparities. It states that at least one study[58] found that the tool performed equally well for Black and Caucasian men (this was a study in which Tim Brennan, COMPAS's creator and chief scientist, was the lead author), but acknowledges that a prior study[59] "reported much weaker results for African American men."[60] In that study, the reliability of the general recidivism tool was only 0.48 for black men.[61] COMPAS suggests that this latter study is unreliable due to the small sample size ($N = 276$).[62]

In 2016, Angwin, Larson, Mattu and Kirchner published a 10,000 subject study on the race effects in the COMPAS tool. Published by ProPublica (and often referred to as the "ProPublica Study"),[63] this study examined actual records drawn from defendants in Broward County, Florida. The results of this study showed "significant racial disparities," it found that COMPAS was "particularly likely to falsely flag black defendants as future criminals," and that "[w]hite defendants were mislabeled as low risk more often than black defendants."[64]

---

58 Brennan (2009).

59 Fass, Heilbrun, DeMatteo and Fretz, (2008).

60 Guide, p. 14.

61 *Ibid.*, p. 14.

62 *Ibid.*

63 This 2016 study was published by ProPublica in an article entitled "Machine Bias: There's Software Used Across the Country to Predict Future Criminals. And it's Biased Against Blacks." (www.propublica.org/article/machine-bias-risk-assessment). The study is often referred to as the "ProPublica study".

64 *Ibid., p.* 3/16. The Angwin study has been subject to a variety of criticisms and analysis which I discuss in detail in Chapter 10.

Usage

The fact that the COMPAS and other tools, have AUC scores of between 0.60 and the low 70s has not stopped their widespread adoption. In any particular case, the ouput of a tool — which is its prediction and risk assessment for an offender — can be over-ridden. That is, a human can determine that the tool's prediction is inaccurate or likely to be inaccurate, and can substitute his own risk determination in its place. But this rarely occurs.

In 2015, the National Center for State Courts published a review of several risk assessment tools in use in 10 jurisdictions across the country.[65] The 10 jurisdictions use both proprietary and non-proprietary instruments. The proprietary instruments include tools from COMPAS, Level of Service Inventory-Revised ("LSI-R"), and Level of Service/Case Management ("LSI/CMI"). The non-proprietary instruments include the Offender Screening Tool ("OST"), the Ohio Risk Assessment System ("ORAS"), and the "Wisconsin Risk Assessment with Strategies for Case Supervision" ("SCS"). The report notes that in all of the 10 jurisdictions, irrespective of instrument used, "accuracy overrides are rarely or never done."[66] The report further notes, however, that "[n]o standard set of measures has formally been proposed to assess the effectiveness of the use of RNA information at sentencing."[67] Moreover, the report notes that comprehensive monitoring of tool usage and results is not consistently in place.[68]

It's possible that the predictions are rarely overridden because the judicial decision-makers are unaware of the AI assessment tools' limited accuracy. A

---

65 J. K. Elek, R. K. Warren, and P. M. Casey, *Using Risk and Needs Assessment Information at Sentencing* (National Center for State Courts, 2015).

66 *Ibid.*, p. 45.

67 *Ibid.*, p. 51.

68 The report states "Most of the 10 jurisdictions interviewed for this report are still in the process of developing a consistent approach to data monitoring and reporting that provides stakeholders with feedback about the effectiveness of local evidence-based sentencing policies and practices" (p. 55). "Because of the length of time that may be required to accumulate a sufficient sample of data, several years may elapses before a jurisdiction is able to fully evaluate longer-term outcomes." *Ibid.*, p. 56.

2015 report from the National Center for State Courts is illustrative. That report includes a quote from a judge who was introduced to AI assessments:

> I've described it to other judges as an epiphany to realize that somebody out there actually realized what worked and what didn't. And there was this whole body of research that I was blissfully ignorant of.... I was instantly interested because I realized that I'd been on the bench, at that point, for 20 years sentencing people, and I really had no clue what I was doing. I didn't know what worked. I didn't know what didn't. I didn't know whether what I was doing was working. So, I thought, yeah, there's all this information out there. We need to learn it, we need to use it.[69]

Prosecutors and judges have both acknowledged the influence of a defendant's RNA score on whether they propose incarceration or that the defendant be allowed to return to the community.[70]

Risk assessment tools are human creations embedded with our biases and assumptions. We see this in the choice of theoretical models, categorizations, and typologies. We see that the tools use data embedded with our human history. When our history provides an immutable narrative of structural inequalities, use of that data to inform predictions about the future makes the past a very real prologue.

What's more is that we still do not know how even the most dissected AI assessment tool, COMPAS, works. We know it contains machine learning, but not what type, where, or how. It is the definition of opacity. Crucially, we also know that the tools are not accurate enough to be used with confidence. A Black man should be very concerned about the use COMPAS and similar risk assessment tools in connection with any liberty decision for him. And all of us should be concerned that we have deployed frequently inaccurate tools across the country to be used in connection with liberty decisions.

---

69 *Ibid.*, p. 4.

70 *Ibid.*, p. 11, 12.

But we can't forget that judges make the ultimate decision as to whether to deprive a person of his liberty. The US Constitution guides that decision-making process. Still, it is not an answer to the inadequacies of AI risk assessment tools to say that they are only informational and merely provide data to the actual human decision-maker, especially when the human decision-maker does not know their limitations.

Fairness at an individual level requires reviewing an offender's current circumstances and, based on that, assessing risks posed. There is an essential unfairness in using a tool that is predisposed to find that the world into which a person was born renders him a likely recidivist.

Chapter 9

COMPAS is Not Alone: Other AI Risk Assessment Tools

⚖

The foregoing analysis of COMPAS might suggest that AI risk assessment tools are approached with caution by court systems. This is not the case. They have, in fact, been wholly embraced.[1]

In 2015, the National Center for State Courts (NCSC) published a report encouraging states to adopt and use the current generation (AI) risk assessment tools in connection with sentencing.[2] The Report was created as part of an initiative financed by the Pew Charitable Trusts to advance "fiscally sound, data-driven policies and practices in sentencing and corrections that protect public safety, hold offenders accountable and control corrections costs."[3]

The Report sets out a variety of ways in which such assessments may be of positive assistance. It also provides what is effectively testimonial support from judges and prosecutors.[4] Missing from the Report is any description of some

---

1   In 2011, the Conference of Chief Justices and the Conference of State Court Administrators adopted a resolution recommending that "offender risk and needs assessment information be available to inform judicial decisions regarding effective management and reduction of risk of offender recidivism." (P. M. Casey and J. K. Elek, *Use of Risk and Needs Assessment Information at Sentencing: La Crosse County*, Wisconsin (National Center for State Courts, 2014).) The Conference referred to such tools "to review whether the defendant can be released prior to adjudication" and also for use "at the plea negotiation stage" (P. M. Casey and J. K. Elek, *Use of Risk and Needs Assessment Information at Sentencing: La Crosse County*, Wisconsin (National Center for State Courts, 2014) p. 2) and at sentencing (*Ibid.*, p. 5). A report on the experience of the court system in La Crosse, Wisconsin identifies COMPAS as in use as of 2012 (prior to that time, a different proprietary instrument had been used, called the Level of Service Inventory-Revised (LSI-R)).

2   J. K. Elek, R. K. Warren, and P. M. Casey, *Using Risk and Needs Assessment Information at Sentencing: Observations from Ten Jurisdictions* (National Center for State Courts, 2015).

3   *Ibid.* (cover page).

4   *Ibid.*, p. 4, 6, 7, 10, 11, et seq.

of the potentially troubling issues we have identified with regard to the COMPAS tool in the prior chapter.

The Report's proffered reason for encouraging use of RNA tools is that they serve a "Public Safety/Risk Management Purpose,"[5] and that the utility of a tool in a sentencing decision is "to inform public safety considerations related to offender risk reduction and management."[6] While the Report cautions that AI tools should not be used as an aggravating or mitigating factor in determining the severity of an offender's sanction,[7] it is hard to see how their outputs could be disregarded. If an offender receives a score that suggests he is at a high risk of committing a violent act, it would be difficult for a judge to ignore that in sentencing and use it only, for instance, to inform whether anger management training is appropriate.

The Report further encourages all jurisdictions to engage in "routine use of assessments ... at all stages of the sentencing process, *including plea bargaining.*"[8] The Report gives illustrations of other ways in which its users find it useful — including in initial decisions prosecutors make about whether (or not) to seek a sentence of incarceration:

> The judge and prosecutor interviewees who have been most involved in EDA [early defendant analysis/aka risk assessment tool analysis] implementation find the program helpful. A prosecutor, for example, expresses trust in the EDA process and believes the RNA information is most beneficial in those prison presumptive cases *in which the prosecution is undecided at the outset whether to offer a non-prison sentence* or has little or no experience with the offender... the prosecutor also acknowledges the tension between the twin goals of accountability [for the crime] and recidivism reduction...[9]

---

5   *Ibid.*, p. 5.

6   *Ibid.*

7   *Ibid.*

8   *Ibid.*, p. 27. (emphasis my own)

9   *Ibid.*, 10. (emphasis my own)

In other words, an assessment score can sometimes help determine whether a defendant receives a plea or sentence with or without jail time. The score can, quite literally, influence a prosecutor to offer incarceration or freedom; the stakes don't get much higher.

The Report further encourages use of risk assessments in connection with determining "Effective Conditions of Probation and Responses to Violations,"[10] which means that the scores and should aid the judge in "crafting terms and conditions of probation supervision that enhance risk reduction."[11] The Report also indicates that in the majority of jurisdictions surveyed in which probation departments are using these tools to predict recidivism, judges are not challenging those recommendations: "A judge in one jurisdiction estimated, for example, that he follows the agency's recommendations in 75–80% of the cases."[12] This is so despite the acknowledgement in the Report that there is confusion between an offender's risk level and his level of actual dangerousness, and perhaps overencouraging the dispensation of prison sentences:

> One of the most common observations on the use of RNA information was that some stakeholders erroneously confuse risk of dangerousness, or think that a high risk score automatically suggests a prison sentence.[13]

These observations highlight a danger: that AI assessment tools are in fact being used by judges, probation officers, and prosecutors as revealing alleged "truths" concerning an offender. There is no indication that the assessments are understood as mere predictions of approximately 60% accuracy. Rather, they are taken as magic 8-balls, harbingers of truth that permit a relinquishment of some crucial discretion.

---

10 *Ibid.*, p. 13.

11 *Ibid.*

12 *Ibid.*, p. 15. See also *Ibid.*, p. 29 (courts typically follow the recommendations in pre-sentence reports that contain risk assessment information generated by these tools).

13 *Ibid.*, p. 30.

LS/CMI

Like COMPAS, the LS/CMI tool is widely used,[14] particularly throughout California and in Canada.[15] It similarly evaluates dozens of factors in connection with a holistic review of both risk and offender need.[16] Like COMPAS, its designers publish a brochure for users, but the LS/CMI version is not nearly as detailed.[17]

LS/CMI relies on information about an offender compiled from several sources, including, as COMPAS does, a structured interview. LS/CMI advertises as a competitive advantage the speed at which the tool can be used and its output generated. What distinguishes LS/CMI is the data-gathering interview's short duration: it can be accomplished in a half hour or less.[18] This is marketed as a selling point for the tool rather than a worrisome characteristic.[19] The tool "refines and combines" 54 items using an undisclosed process.[20]

Also like COMPAS, the LS/CMI instrument is theory driven. It is grounded in a selection of criminological theoretical frameworks: "a mix of static and dynamic factors, developed from recidivism literature."[21] From an accuracy standpoint, the LS/CMI tool fares no better than COMPAS. A report

---

14 D. A. Andrews, J. Bonta and J. S. Wormith, "The Recent Past and Near Future of Risk and/ or Need Assessment", *Crime & Delinquency*, 52(1), 7–27, (2006). doi: https://doi.org/10.1177/0011128705281756.

15 T. Agnese and S. Curran, "The California Risk Assessment Pilot Project: The Use of Risk and Needs Assessment Information in Adult Felony Probation Sentencing and Violation Proceedings" (2015), www. publicsafety.gc.ca/rsk-nd-rspnsvty/index-en.

16 Z. Hamilton, A. Kigerl, M. Campagna, R. Barnoski, S. Lee, nJ. van Wormer, and L. Block, "Designed to Fit", *Criminal Justice and Behavior*, 43(2), (2015), doi: https://doi.org/10.1177/0093854815615633; LSCMI_Tech_Brochure).

17 www.gifrinc.com/product/ls-cmi; see also https://www.youtube.com/channel/UCGcgUBUpVZ6Dgdkb7hhaZdA.

18 www.gifrinc.com/product/ls-cmi.

19 www.storefront.mhs.com.

20 www.pccd.pa.gov/funding/document/ls-cmi-pccd.

21 *Ibid.*

commissioned by the Oregon Criminal Justice Commission and published in June 2019[22] found AUC scores of 0.63.[23]

One validation study of the tool, focused on Nebraska, found that there is a "significant interaction of overall LS/CMI risk level and minority status, which means that the instrument predicts recidivism somewhat differently for minorities than non-minorities."[24] The report states: "Although the predictive power for general recidivism for the LS/CMI appears to be slightly better for non-minorities in Nebraska, the difference is small and significant mainly due to the large sample size of the analysis."[25] In comparing the results of the Nebraska study to those of other parts of the country, the authors found that it performed about the same for minorities in the rest of the country.[26]

In 2015, a joint project of the Judicial Council of California, the State Justice Institute, and the National Institute for Corrections sponsored a report analyzing the results of California's risk assessment pilot project. Given that California used (and continues to use) LS/CMI, it included a specific review of the tool.[27] This report compiled results from four pilot sites: Napa, San Francisco, Santa Cruz and Yolo Counties.[28] The examination coincided with a larger statewide effort to reduce incarceration, making it hard to distinguish between results attributable to use of the tool and overall policy considerations. In general, these counties reported that they "significantly reduced their combined probation failure rate (PFR) and sentenced a significantly lower

---

22 S. Radakrishnan, W. Campbell, M. Brune, and K. Neary, "Oregon LS/CMI Assessment Final Report" (2019.

23 *Ibid.*, p. 46.

24 R. Wiener, K. Reed, R. H. Delgado, and A. Caldwell, "Validation Study of the LS/CMI Assessment Tool in Nebraska", Technical Report (2014), p. 26, DOI: 10.13140/RG.2.2.33171.99364.

25 *Ibid.*, p. 30.

26 *Ibid.*

27 Agnese and Curran (2015).

28 Napa County uses a series of tools including the LS/CMI tool for general recidivism, a specialized risk assessment tool for domestic violence ("SARA"), a tool for sex offenders and one for substance abuse. (A-12, "Using Risk and Needs Assessment Information at Sentencing: Observations from Ten Jurisdictions, (2015).)

proportion of felony probationers to prison and jail compared to jurisdictions in the rest of the state."[29] The effects of the LS/CMI tool and the simultaneous statewide initiative were not separated.[30]

The California Report concluded in bold: "the use of evidence-based presentence investigation reports at sentencing proceedings and evidence-based supplemental/ violation reports at violation proceedings results in improved felony probationer outcomes compared to the use of evidence-based supervision practices alone."[31] The report also tracked the "level of implementation" of the LS/CMI tool within the state: between 2011 and 2014, utilization throughout the state had increased dramatically.[32] Finally, the report found that since 2011, a "larger proportion of judges report that they had confidence that EBP [evidence-based-practices/ risk assessment tools] help to reduce recidivism" (rising from 54% to 65%).[33] The evidence of widening adoption and use occurs despite AUC levels in the low 60s and demonstrable race-based differences in output.

Other Tools Used by States

Other assessment tools in wide use include the Ohio Risk Assessment Instrument (ORAS) and the ONA/Strong-R tools. ORAS was initially developed in Ohio and is now licensed to a number of other states, including Texas, Florida, and Indiana.[34]

Over time, the ONA tool evolved into the STRONG assessment system, which is a custom designed system now deployed in Washington State. The acronym "STRONG-R" is drawn from two prior instruments used in the State: a static risk (STR) and Offender Needs Guide (ONG). STRONG-R was first utilized in 2013.

---

29 *Ibid.*, p. 8.

30 *Ibid.*, p. 7.

31 *Ibid.*, p. 21.

32 *Ibid.*, p. 53 (in 2011 usage hovered around 57%, by 2014 usage had increased to over 80%).

33 *Ibid.*, p. 55.

34 Z. Hamilton, A. Kigerl, M. Campagna, R. Barnoski, S. Lee, J. van Wormer, and L. Block, "Designed to Fit: The Development and Validation of Strong-R Recidivism Risk Assessment", *Criminal Justice and Behavior* (2015), https://doi.org/10.1177/0093854815615633.

STRONG-R scores 140 separate items.[35] Unlike the COMPAS tool, we do not know the criminological theories underlying STRONG-R's input selection. The input categories, which we do know, are necessarily reflective of some human individual's theoretical judgments, but whose?

Among STRONG-R's input categories[36] are factors that are often associated with structural racism and racial stereotypes including longest period of employment, antisocial friendships, friends in a gang, residential status (stable, transitional, homeless), occupants of a residence (including antisocial friends), family prior criminal problems, aggressive motivations, and attitude/behavior towards authority figures.[37] STRONG-R's predictive validity has been measured with AUC scores ranging from 0.63 to 0.78.[38]

States across the country use a number of different tools that have developed without standardization as to input content, weighting adjustment, methodology, or interpretation. Reported validation statistics indicate variability between these tools of up to 0.10 or more. Moreover, studies that have carefully examined tools for race effects have found them. Yet these assessment tools are used every day to make predictions about a person's behavior that influences the liberty decision-making of judges and prosecutors. While there is an argument that these tools may prove useful for programming choices as related to education, job training, or anger management, there are layers of unfairness pertaining to incarceration that overrides other forms of use.

The Federal Tool: PCRA

While the federal system is based in a different jurisdiction, its risk and need assessment practices don't vary widely from the state courts.[39] Like state judges, federal judges routinely make pre-trial bail and sentencing determinations. In

---

35 *Ibid.*, p. 246.

36 *Ibid.*, p. 241.

37 *Ibid.*, pp. 241–243.

38 *Ibid.*, pp. 250–251.

39 Within the United States, there are separate but parallel federal and state court systems.

connection with such decisions, federal judges receive input from pre-trial and probation officers. Also like the state system, the federal system has sought to reduce variability in liberty determinations and has used forms of actuarial risk assessment for post-conviction supervision since the 1920s.[40]

Over time, software and data advances have led to the development of new and more sophisticated tools. In 2004, the Judicial Conference of the United States adopted a strategic approach to reduce recidivism. It tasked the main administrative office for the federal court system, referred to as the "Administrative Office" or "AO," to develop an evidence-based approach to post-conviction supervision. The AO established pilot programs in five jurisdictions to evaluate three proprietary tools already in use in state systems: LS/CMI, COMPAS and a third system, Risk Assessment Systems (RMS).[41] Ultimately, the AO determined that "creating an instrument with data specific to the federal probation system was preferable."[42]

The AO developed a bespoke tool that it deployed in 2011 called Post Conviction Risk Assessment (PCRA).[43] PCRA determines a risk level based on the "presence or absence of criminogenic factors" including "personal characteristics and circumstances statistically associated with an increased chance of recidivism."[44] Like other assessment tools, it views "antisocial attitudes, antisocial associates, impulsivity, substance abuse, and deficits in educational, vocational, and employment skills" as contributing to criminal conduct.[45] It is modeled on the belief that though "static factors such as criminal history are

---

40   J. L. Johnson, C. T. Lowenkamp, S. W. VanBenschoten, and C. R. Robinson, "The Construction and Validation of Federal Post Conviction Risk Assessment", *Federal Probation*, 75(2) (2011), 17.

41   The "Risk Assessment System" is associated with the tool that became the Ohio Risk Assessment System, discussed above. It is a basic package of tools that can be customized.

42   J. L. Johnson, C. T. Lowenkamp, S. W. VanBenschoten, and C. R. Robinson, "The Construction and Validation of the Federal Post Conviction Risk Assessment (PCRA)", *Federal Probation*, 75(2) (2011), 18.

43   *Ibid.*

44   *Ibid.*

45   *Ibid.*

good predictors of offending, they do not identify what needs should be targeted to reduce reoffending."[46]

The data used to construct and validate PCRA was drawn from five pilot federal districts that had been testing discarded commercial tools. An early validation study of PCRA included a sample of over 190,000 offenders and had AUCs ranging from 0.70 to 0.78.[47] These AUCs "plac[ed] it among the most accurate instruments in the field of criminal risk and needs assessment."[48] PCRA 2.0 was deployed in 2014 and included a prediction of violent recidivism. A 2016 validation study resulted in AUCs of between 0.73 and 0.74.[49]

Similar to other instruments we have discussed, PCRA is based heavily on an interview and a self-assessment. It originally included both scored and non-scored items.[50] Scored items are typically direct contributors to the risk score for an offender; unscored items are informational and also used to assess recommended programming and services to reduce recidivism and address an offender's needs. Certain scored items were removed from the original tool with no material impact on predictive accuracy.[51]

The selection of academic research, by individuals unknown and undisclosed, plays a significant role in the tool's design:

> Scored items have been demonstrated by the Administrative Office's empirical research to be statistically significant predictors of recidivism, and they contribute to the tool's final conclusion regarding risk level and

---

46 *Ibid.*

47 *Ibid., p.* 21.

48 "The Federal Post Conviction Risk Assessment (PCRA): A Construction and Validation Study," (2012) (available at www.uscourts.gov/postconviction-risk-assessment).

49 J. Luallen, S. Radakrishnan, and W. Rhodes, "The Predictive Validity of the Post-Conviction Risk Assessment Among Federal Offenders", *Criminal Justice and Behavior* (2016) (www.doj.org/10.1177/0093854816650481).

50 *Ibid.*, p. 10.

51 T. H. Cohen and K. Bechtel, "Removal of Non-Scored Items from the Post-Conviction Risk Assessment Instrument: An Evaluation of Data-driven Risk Assessment Research Within the Federal System", *Probation Risk Assessment*, 81(2) (2017).

criminogenic needs. Unscored items have been shown by other empirical research to be predictors of recidivism but have not been studied by the Administrative Office in federal cases due to the lack of necessary data. They are included for data collection purposes and to inform the instrument's final conclusion regarding criminogenic needs and responsivity factors (barriers to supervision and treatment), but not risk level.[52]

PCRA 2.0 contains 25 scored and 38 unscored items. Among the factors included are: criminal history, age, highest level of education, employment status, drug use history, marital status, family stability, the nature of the person's relationship with peers, whether a weapon was used in the offense, and prior history of violence. The most indefinite factors are those in the "responsivity domain." Among these are low intelligence, no desire to change/participate in programs, and ethnic/cultural barriers.[53]

The self-assessment portion of the study (called "PICTS") is intended to elucidate an offender's "thinking style" and includes whether he tends to project blame on external factors such as upbringing, poverty, or the government.[54] Some of the answers in the PICTS part of the study are simple "yes" or "no" answers.

The combination of the officer interview and self-assessment produce an output page that set forth risk categories for general and violent recidivism as well as a description of criminogenic needs. In some circumstances, users can deviate from the PCRA scoring by employing an "override" function.[55]

Unlike other tools, the use of PCRA has been standardized and is limited to those who have received and passed certification training. Prior to receiving

---

52 L. Johnson, and R. van Benschoten, "The Construction and Validation of Federal Post Conviction Risk Assessment", *Federal Probation Journal*, 75(2), pp. 25–29, (2011).

53 *Ibid.*

54 *Ibid.*

55 *Ibid.*

certification, potential users are tested on their ability to accurately record information from assessments and to interpret risk and need scoring.

As with other AI risk assessment tools, studies of PCRA demonstrate that its current algorithmic design results in race discrepancies: predictive accuracy is higher for white than Black offenders.[56] Skeem and Lowenkamp suggest alternative algorithm design to address some of these effects.[57] It remains to be seen whether a redesigned PCRA utilizing Skeem and Lowenkamp's suggestions will be deployed.

In sum, the AO has spent considerable time designing an algorithmic assessment tool specific to the needs of the federal system. And while specific attention has been paid to fairness and equity issues, the tool's design results in some of the same inherent utilitarian issues we have seen with other tools.

56 J. Skeem and C. T. Lowenkamp, "Using Algorithms to Address Trade-Offs Inherent in Predicting Recidivism," *Behavioral Sciences & The Law*, 38(1) (2020).

57 *Ibid.*, pp. 9–11.

Chapter 10
Accuracy over Fairness

⚖

Ve have spent a great deal of this book considering the fundamental unfairness of AI tools that extrapolate from patterned behavior to make determinations on a specific individual's liberty. No defendant should be sentenced for the criminal conduct or propensities of another; the sins of the father should not be attributed to the son. These utilitarian tools are innately ill-suited for our founding theories of justice, but they are particularly pernicious when they yield demonstrably different results based on race.

This chapter explores the evolution of the debate regarding racial unfairness in these tools. What began as a denial that the tools were racially biased quickly moved to acceptance. One might imagine that acceptance would have resulted in an immediate recognition that these tools cannot be used for liberty decisions. But, instead, acceptance has been paired with a re-articulation of the goal of RNAs: achieving the highest degree of accuracy for an overall population regardless of fairness at the individual level. Justice demands more.

AI enabled risk assessment tools are riddled with a particularly nefarious potential: their algorithms can render structural unfairness self-reinforcing. That is, the very facts underlying historic and present-day structural unfairness are used in the model as factors indicating higher risk or criminality, thereby baking bias into the data set even as we may move consciously into more fair policing and prosecutorial practices. This has serious implications for the personal liberty of any defendant who exists within a system of entrenched discrimination, with particular consequences for Black defendants.

The AI model does not allow timely flexibility based on increased awareness of the need for social change. Judges who might be influenced by increased awareness of structural inequities brought about, for instance, by the Black Lives Matter Movement, are nonetheless presented with a risk score that cannot and does not take any of that into consideration. The danger of this is that at least some judges will defer to the scientific claims of the model, ignoring that those claims are inexorably tethered to a set of structural inequalities.

The Evolution of the Debate

Long before risk assessment tools began to be widely adopted in court systems across the country,[1] COMPAS understood racial discrepancies in predictive accuracy. A 2008 study found that COMPAS's predictive accuracy differed by ethnic group.[2] It found that in predicting re-arrest the AUC for Blacks was only *0.48*, compared to 0.81 for whites. COMPAS dismissed the results as based on an overly small sample size of 276,[3] but an AUC of 0.48 should have resulted in red flashing lights that something was terribly wrong. A 2009 study yielded contrary results, finding that COMPAS's models performed equally well for Blacks and whites.[4] But this new study was hardly objective: the study was validated by none other than COMPAS's own founder, Tim Brennan.[5]

---

1   The first generation of risk assessment tools is considered to be human, or clinical judgment, alone. In the 1920s, a second-generation tool (called the "Burgess Scale") that statistically modeled unweighted actuarial factors began to be used. In the 1970s, Wisconsin introduced a third-generation tool with a classification tool that used static information about an offender but introduced dynamic risk factors. This included dynamic factors (such as drug abuse) that were considered subject to change, along with static factors (for instance, age at first arrest). The third-generation tools then evolved further and began to include a form of scoring. Fourth generation tools are defined not by technology but by the inclusion of both risk and needs assessments. The algorithmic sophistication, leading to designation as a form of artificial intelligence, occurred somewhere between the time these tools were first announced and 2012. By then, they were widely viewed as using computational power, large data sets, and sophisticated algorithms that assess patterns and learn in order to assist with output. That is, they became artificially intelligent in a basic sense. Their sophistication has grown over time. The algorithms and methods of learning/training the models are now generally maintained as confidential by the designers and not disclosed. "Risk/Needs Assessment: Is This the Best We Can Do?", *Federal Probation*, 72(2) (2008) (www.uscourts.gov/sites/default/risk needs assessment).

2   Fass, Heilbrun, DeMatteo, and Fretz (2008).

3   Guide, p. 14.

4   Brennan (2009).

5   Brennan is currently the Chief Scientist at Northpointe, Inc., the owner of the COMPAS tool.

As usage became more widespread, so did concerns about racial bias in tool output. An explosive article in May 2016 by Angwin, Larson, Mattu, and Kirchner, published by ProPublica, shone a spotlight on racial differences.[6] Angwin *et al.*, performed a comprehensive study and minced no words in presenting their findings: COMPAS produced biased results for Black defendants. Angwin and her colleagues used a straightforward methodology: they obtained risk scores assigned by COMPAS in 2013 and 2014 to 7000 arrestees from Broward County, Florida. They then compared those scores in 2016 to the arrestees' subsequent actual histories. In short, they compared the pediction with the reality.

As a general matter, the Angwin Study found that COMPAS was not particularly accurate for anyone, and that it calculated a risk score that "proved remarkably unreliable in forecasting violent crime: Only 20% of the people predicted to commit violent crimes actually went on to do so."[7] When all variations of criminal behavior were taken into account (including misdemeanors as minor as driving with an expired license), the tool was slightly more accurate than a coin flip. Even more importantly, the study "also turned up significant racial disparities"[8]:

- "The [algorithm] was particularly likely to falsely flag black defendants as future criminals, wrongly labeling them this way at *almost twice the rate* of white defendants."[9]
- "White defendants were mislabeled as low risk more often than black defendants."
- Angwin *et al.* ran a statistical analysis that they said was designed to isolate the effect of race from criminal history, recidivism, age and gender. They found that Black defendants were still 77% more likely to be "pegged as

---

6   www.propublica.org/article/machine-bias-risk-assessments-in-criminal-sentencing.

7   Angwin, p. 3/16. This 2016 study was published by ProPublica in an article entitled "Machine Bias: There's Software Used Across the Country to Predict Future Criminals. And it's Biased Against Blacks." (www.propublica.org/article/machine-bias-risk-assessment). The study is often referred to as the "ProPublica study".

8   *Ibid.*, p. 3/16.

9   *Ibid.*, (emphasis added).

at higher risk of committing a future violent crime and 45% more likely to be predicted to commit a future crime of any kind."[10]

The study focused on a few examples of egregious errors. In the first, a young black woman with no prior criminal history was arrested for the minor theft of an $80 bike. Her COMPAS score indicated that she was at high risk of recidivism. In contrast, at about the same time, a 41-year-old white man who had a criminal history that included a felony conviction for armed robbery for which he had served several years in prison, was convicted for stealing approximately $80 of goods from a Home Depot. He had a low risk categorization by COMPAS. Two years later, the young woman had no further arrests and the man was serving an 8-year prison term for a new offense: stealing thousands of dollars of electronics from a warehouse.[11]

Ultimately, Angwin and her colleagues concluded that the COMPAS prediction fails according to race. 44.9% of Black offenders were labeled higher risk but didn't reoffend, while only 23.5% of whites were. The converse was also true: 47.7% of whites were labeled lower risk but did reoffend, while only 28.0% of Black offenders that had been labeled lower risk in fact reoffended.[12]

Northpointe's Immediate Response

COMPAS's owner, Northpointe, responded to Angwin et al. within six weeks with a study from its own research department.[13] Among the researchers on the team was Tim Brennan.

The Northpointe report — "COMPAS Risk Scales: Demonstrating Accuracy Equity and Predictive Parity" published on July 8, 2016 — described an unsuccessful attempt to replicate the analysis performed by Angwin and her

---

10 *Ibid.*, pp. 3–4/16.

11 *Ibid.*, p. 2/16.

12 *Ibid.*, p. 11/16.

13 www.volarisgroup.com/430-MBX-989/demonstrating-accuracy-equity.

colleagues.[14] This exercise persuaded the Northpointe team that Angwin and her colleagues had made a number of errors. Most significantly, they asserted that Angwin's statistics failed to take into account the "different base rates of recidivism for blacks and whites."[15] This was revealing. It is a key acknowledgement that since the records used to populate the initial database reflect higher arrest and conviction rates for Black people, there will always be certain racial differences in the tool's output. Another less charitable translation of this is that Northpointe views the data as accurately reflecting that Black people are over-represented in crime statistics, and that because they have been arrested more frequently than whites, they in fact commit more crime, and their chances of recidivism are higher. This position accepts structural inequalities as a permanent fixture, and racially biased policing and prosecutorial policies and practices as reflective of actual criminal conduct. The reality is different: Black Americans have been arrested and convicted at rates disproportionate to their representation in the population.[16] In the absence of structural equalities and embedded racism, nothing suggests that Black people would commit crimes at anything other than a proportionate rate.

The rationale that COMPAS has given to the issue — "it's just the data"; "the facts are what they are" — has been repeated in various iterations in every study that has defended race discrepancies produced by assessment tools. This justification is even included in COMPAS's 2019 version of its Guide.

According to the Northpointe research team, once the correct data and methodology was applied, they were able to achieve "accuracy equity" and predictive parity for Black and white offenders.[17] The report continues:

> [A]s the mean difference in scores between the low-scoring group and a high scoring group is increased, the base rates diverge and higher false positive rates and lower false negative rates are obtained for the higher scoring

---

14 W. Dieterich, C. Mendoza, and T. Brennan, "COMPAS Risk Scales: Demonstrating Accuracy Equity and Predictive Parity", Northpointe Research Departmentt (2016).

15 *Ibid.*, p. 1.

16 M. Alexander, *The New Jim Crow: Mass Incarceration in the Age of Colorblindness*(The New Press, 2010), pp. 180–181.

17 Guide, Exec. Summary.

group. This is the same pattern of results reported by Angwin *et al.* This pattern does *not* show evidence of bias, but rather is the natural consequence of using unbiased scoring rules for groups that happen to have different distribution scores.[18]

It is useful to translate this. This paragraph can be understood as saying the following: Black offenders tend to score as higher risk on the recidivism scales than white offenders; as scores diverge, the models predict that higher scoring offenders are more likely to recidivate; this means that there will be a higher chance of a false positive for a Black offender who is in this higher risk score category, than a white one. Put more bluntly, because the tools use flawed historical data which says that Black people commit more crimes, the tools will often predict that Black offenders are predisposed to criminal behavior and recidivism. Again, past becomes prologue. Black offenders are caught in a cyclical pattern of racism.

In September 2016, the Federal Probation Department published "False Positives, False Negatives, and False Analyses: A Rejoinder to 'Machine Bias: There's Software Used Across the Country to Predict Future Criminals. And It's Biased Against Blacks'" (the "Flores" Study).[19] The authors criticize Angwin's study on the basis that it relies on "faulty statistics and data analysis."[20] They start by suggesting that in fact the criminal justice system itself, but not the assessment tools, may be biased against Black offenders:

> It might be that the existing justice system is biased against poor minorities due to a wide variety of reasons (including economic factors, policing patterns, prosecutorial behavior, and judicial biases).[21]

They further caution that "It would be a shame if policymakers mistakenly thought that risk assessment tools were somehow worse than the status quo" and that "risk assessment tools informed by objective data can help reduce bias from

---

18 *Ibid.*, p. 8.

19 Flores, Bechtel, and Lowenkamp (2016).

20 *Ibid.*, p. 38.

21 *Ibid.*

its current level."[22] Like the Northpointe study, the authors analyze the same data but use a different methodology than Angwin and her colleagues. Their results show slightly better prediction accuracy for Black defendants than white, with an AUC of 0.70 versus 0.69. They criticize the Angwin piece as forcing a "dichotomy on the COMPAS [tool]. The COMPAS was not made to make absolute predictions about success or failure. Instead, it was designed to inform probabilities."[23] While this may be true, it ignores the encouraged and actual uses of the tools: to inform individual decisions on bail, sentencing, and services.

The Flores Study also finds race discrepancies in the COMPAS tool, but not predictive bias. They explain the difference as follows:

> It is important to note that the general recidivism base rate for Black defendants is significantly higher than it is for White defendants specifically, and the overall sample generally. Racial differences in failure rates across race describe the behavior of defendants and the criminal justice system, not assessment bias.[24]

They conclude, "we failed to find evidence of predictive bias in the COMPAS."[25]

A month later, in October 2016, Alexandra Chouldechova, from Carnegie Mellon University, largely found what Flores had found: that COMPAS was free of predictive bias. But Chouldechova posited a different theory: that the difference in scoring for Black and white offenders nevertheless might constitute disparate impact.[26] Chouldechova's study showed that "differences in false positive and false negative rates cited as evidence of racial bias in the ProPublica

---

22 *Ibid.*, p. 38. The study cites to the same studies and meta-analyses as those discussed in the COMPAS Guide for the proposition that "actuarial risk assessments are superior to unstructured professional judgment." (*Ibid.*, p. 39.) For the reasons set forth in the previous chapters, these studies are limited. Citation to these articles has become like an echo-chamber: one study references them, then another picks up the baton, and so on and so forth. They do not become more persuasive or apposite merely by being cited more.

23 *Ibid.*, p. 40.

24 *Ibid.*, P. 41.

25 *Ibid.*, P. 44.

26 A. Chouldechova, "Fair Prediction with Disparate Impact: A Study of Bias in Recidivism Prediction Instruments" (Cornell University, 2016), www.arvix.org/stat/fair-prediction-disparate-impact.

article are a direct consequence of applying an instrument that is free from predictive bias to a population in which recidivism prevalence differs across groups."[27] She argues:

> It is important to bear in mind that fairness itself — along with the notion of disparate impact — is a social and ethical concept, not a statistical one. An instrument that is free from predictive bias may nevertheless result in disparate impact depending on how and where it is used.[28]

Chouldechova then uses the same Broward County data set as that used by Angwin and Northpointe to show that "differences in false positive rates between Black defendants and White defendants persist across prior record subgroups."[29] Thus while the higher rate of false positives for Black defendants may not show intentional bias, Chouldecova posits that it may show disparate impact.[30]

Chouldechova argues that in light of these results, there may be "risk assessment use cases in which it is desirable to balance error rates across different groups, even though this will generally result in risk assessments that are not free from predictive bias."[31] To rephrase, Chouldechova is suggesting that the algorithm may need to be manually altered in order to balance error rates. To do this, she warns, will result in a different form of predictive bias.

A few months after this article, one of the AO's prominent researchers Christopher T. Lowenkamp teamed up with Jennifer Skeem of the University of California at Berkeley to analyze racially-based predictive bias in the PCRA tool.[32] Their study examined a sample of 34,794 federal offenders for any

---

27 *Ibid.*, p. 1.

28 *Ibid.*

29 *Ibid.*, p. 4.

30 *Ibid.*

31 *Ibid.*, p. 5.

32 J. L. Skeem and C. T. Lowenkamp, "Risk, Race & Recidivism: Predictive Bias and Disparate Impact" (Wiley Online Library, 2016), www.ssrn.com/asbtract=2687339).

relationship between race, risk assessment, and future arrest, and it examined four key questions:

(1) to what extent is the instrument — and the risk factors it includes — free of predictive bias?
(2) to what extent does the instrument yield average score differences between racial groups that are relevant to disparate impact?
(3) which risk factors contribute the most and the least to mean score differences between Black and White offenders?
(4) are variables such as criminal history best understood as proxies for race, or mediators of the relationship between race and recidivism?[33]

Their results indicated that PCRA strongly predicts recidivism (with AUCs between 0.70 and 0.78) for both Black and white offenders[34] but that "Black offenders obtain higher average PCRA scores than White offenders, so some applications could create disparate impact."[35] Consistent with several prior studies, they suggested that 66% of this difference is attributable to an actual difference in criminal history between white and Black offenders.[36]

Skeem and Lowenkamp emphasize that PCRA does not include race as a predictive factor. To explain how race discrepancies are nonetheless apparent, they state: "Although race is omitted from these instruments, critics assert that risk factors that are sometimes included (e.g. marital history, employment status) are "proxies" for minority race and poverty."[37] They go on: "Given that young black men are six times more likely to be imprisoned than young white men (Carson, 2015) . . . [r]isk assessment could *exacerbate* racial disparities."[38] Skeem and Lowenkamp ultimately determine that it is, however, possible that

---

33 *Ibid.*, p. 14.

34 *Ibid.*, p. 29.

35 *Ibid.*, p. 2.

36 *Ibid.*, pp. 34–35.

37 *Ibid.*, p. 3.

38 *Ibid.*, p. 4.

use of the tools could have no effect on racial disparities or even reduce them.[39] They acknowledge that concerns regarding potential racial bias in the tools impact all stages of the criminal justice process. If "higher-risk offenders are subject to more intensive community supervision and risk reduction services — and service refusal violates the terms of release — they are more subject to social control than their lower-risk counterparts."[40]

Skeem and Lowenkamp further acknowledge that race and criminal history are correlated, with Black defendants having higher average criminal history scores than whites:

> Criminal history reflects not only the differential participation of racial groups in crime (e.g. Black people being involved in crime — particularly violent/serious crime — at a higher rate than Whites), but also the differential selection of given groups by criminal justice officials (e.g., police decisions about arrest; prosecutor decisions about charging) and by sentencing policies (e.g., minimum mandatories...) The proportion of racial disparities in crime explained by differential participation vs. differential selection is hotly debated... and varies as a function of crime type (e.g., violence vs. drug crimes) and stage of justice processing (e.g., arrest vs. incarceration).[41]

For Skeem and Lowenkamp:

> [A]ny instrument used to inform sentencing must be shown to predict recidivism with similar accuracy across groups. If the instrument is unbiased, a given score will also have the same meaning regardless of group membership (e.g., an average risk score of X will relate to an average recidivism rate of Y for *both* Black and White groups.)[42]

According to even Skeem and Lowenkamp, there cannot be true predictive parity. They attribute the reasons for this to:

---

39 *Ibid.*

40 *Ibid.*, p. 5.

41 *Ibid.*, pp. 8–9 (internal citations omitted).

42 *Ibid.*, p. 10.

[L]ongstanding patterns of social and economic inequality in the U.S. (e.g., differences in social networks/resources, neighborhoods, education, employment). Although poverty and inequality do not inevitably lead to crime, they "involve circumstances that do contribute to criminal behavior." (Walker, Spohn, and DeLone, 2011, p. 99). Group differences in such circumstances can manifest as valid group differences in risk scores.[43]

Thus, as Skeem and Lowenkamp state, an instrument can perform perfectly — it can measure real risk and produce reliable results — but nevertheless fail an essential test of fairness.[44] They therefore advise that instruments and the risk factors that they incorporate must be "empirically examined for both predictive bias and disparate impact. Simply put, risk assessments must be both empirically valid and perceived as morally fair across groups."[45]

The ultimate concern, as Skeen and Lowencamp clarify, is that while risk assessments have the potential to "unwind mass incarceration without compromising public safety," certain uses of the tool can actually exacerbate racial disparities in incarceration.[46] They pose the following dilemma: "If one concern — predictive accuracy or social justice — is valued to the exclusion of the other, there is no dilemma. But if both concerns are valued — which is most likely — the two goals must be balanced."[47] As a result, they recommend that instruments be examined for bias at both the test and input level, but caution that "[i]f policymakers blindly eradicate risk factors from a tool because they are contentious, they risk reducing predictive utility *and* exacerbating the racial disparities they seek to ameliorate."[48] They conclude by stating that the instrument is only part of an overall equation in sentencing, and that there is a human element that can add racial bias as well: "There is no empirical basis for assuming that the status quo — across contexts — is preferable to judicious

---

43 *Ibid.*, p. 11.

44 *Ibid.*

45 *Ibid.*

46 *Ibid.*, p. 36.

47 *Ibid.*

48 *Ibid.*, pp.36–37.

application of a well-validated and unbiased risk assessment instrument. We hope the field proceeds with due caution."[49]

The Fairness Debate

At the end of 2016, Kleinberg, Mullainathan, and Raghavan acknowledged the debate about AI tools and race and began to turn it towards questions of fairness: "Recent discussion in the public sphere about algorithmic classifications has involved tensions between competing notions of what it means for probabilistic classification to be fair to different groups."[50]

Kleinberg *et al.* understand that the essential tension in moving from the data set to the individual: "[A] growing line of work has asked how we should reason about issues of bias and discrimination in settings where these algorithmic and statistical techniques, trained on large datasets of past instances, play a significant role in the outcome."[51] The Kleinberg Study explains that while Angwin identified asymmetric errors (Black offenders were more likely to be labeled as higher-risk than they actually were, while white offenders were more likely to be incorrectly labeled as lower-risk than they actually were), the tools were in fact producing "true" outcomes.[52] They identify as a goal "that … probability estimates should have the same effectiveness regardless of group membership."[53] That is, accuracy predictions should perform equally well for both Black and white people. But as of today, they acknowledge, this is not achievable and "can only be simultaneously satisfied in highly constrained cases."[54]

It's useful to distill these results further. The Kleinberg study finds that as long as the historical data reflects Black people being arrested at disproportionate rates, the AI assessment tools will carry that pattern forward and predict higher

49 *Ibid.*, p. 38.

50 Abstract, "Inherent Trade-Offs in the Fair Determination of Risk Scores" (2016).

51 *Ibid.*, p. 1.

52 *Ibid.*

53 *Ibid.*, p. 3.

54 *Ibid.*, p. 3.

rates of recidivism.[55] The study concludes by acknowledging that "there may be a number of settings in which the cost (social or otherwise) of false positives may differ greatly from the cost of false negatives."[56] In other words, if society rejects risk assessment tools that unfairly and incorrectly predict the criminality of Black people, then the models can be changed — or as the study articulates it, the "models might be subject to calibration."[57]

In the following years, debates regarding race differentials of AI risk assessment tools have continued to probe questions of fairness.

In 2018, Dressel and Farid performed a study of the predictive accuracy of humans making individualized determinations versus machines that use aggregate historical data.[58] Their bottom line is that humans are, in fact, just as good as machines at making predictions about human behavior (even humans without particular expertise). They used, as their exemplar, the COMPAS tool.

In order to conduct the study, Dressel and Farid provided human subjects with facts about an offender and information about the crime he or she committed; they did not, however, provide humans with the offender's race. Meanwhile, the researchers provided COMPAS with the same background information as the humans, and also provided the tool with the offender's race. The study therefore operationalized 'offender's race' as the independent variable. With these preconditions, the authors found that humans incorrectly predicted recidivism for Black offenders — that is, they returned false positives — at a rate of 37.1%; COMPAS had a false positive rate of 40.4% for the same offenders. Similarly, humans incorrectly predicted that Black offenders would not recidivate — that is, they returned false negatives — at a rate of 29.2%; COMPAS returned false negatives at a 30.9% rate for the same offenders. In terms of white offenders, humans returned false positives at a rate of 27.2% and false negatives at a rate of 40.3%. For the same offenders, COMPAS

---

55 *Ibid.*, p. 17.

56 *Ibid.*

57 *Ibid.*

58 J. Dressel and H. Farid, "The Accuracy, Fairness and Limits of Predicting Recidivism", *Science Advances*, 4(1) (2018) eaao5580, DOI: 10.1126/sciadv.aao5580.

returned false positive and negative rates of 25.4% and 47.9%, respectively. Clearly, when race is removed from the equation, humans are at least as capable as COMPAS in predicting recidivism or lack thereof. And, when it comes to false negatives for white offenders, humans are perhaps more accurate. In further analysis, the authors found that despite the complexity of the COMPAS tool, only two factors — age and total number of prior convictions — were necessary to arrive at the same predictive conclusions:

> When considering using software such as COMPAS in making decisions that will significantly affect the lives and well-being of criminal defendants, it is valuable to ask whether we would put these decisions in the hands of random people who respond to an online survey because, in the end, the results from these two approaches appear to be indistinguishable.[59]

In 2018, another group of researchers, Berk, Heidari, Jabbari, Kearns, and Roth, also published a study focusing on fairness in RNAs.[60] They found that there are at least "six kinds of fairness" and that a major complication to achieving fairness using existing tools relates to differences in the "base rates across legally protected groups."[61] In their view, "an overall conclusion will be that you can't have it all. Rhetoric to the contrary, challenging tradeoffs are required between different kinds of fairness and between fairness and accuracy."[62] They articulate the problem bluntly:

> The implications of the impossibility results are huge. First, if there is variation in base rates and no separation, you can't have it all. The goal of complete race or gender neutrality is unachievable. In practice, both requirements are virtually never met, except in highly stylized examples.[63]

This lack of neutrality is a difficult problem to fix. As the authors acknowledge, "altering a risk algorithm to improve matters can lead to difficult stakeholder

---

59 *Ibid.*, p. 3.

60 R. Berk, H. Heidari, S. Jabbari, M. Kearns, and A. Roth, "Fairness in Criminal Justice Risk Assessments: the State of the Art", *Sociological Methods and Research* (2018), https://doi.org/10.1177/0049124118782533.

61 *Ibid.*, pp. 13–16.

62 *Ibid.*, p. 3.

63 *Ibid.*, p. 18.

choices."[64] They tested alterations in weightings and found that if you start manipulating the weights, you may have results that appear to achieve predictive equality, but that are fundamentally inaccurate. The results therefore do not give the user sufficient information regarding what type of treatment may reduce chances of recidivism: "Different base rates across protected group categories would seem to require a thumb on the scale if conditional use equality is to be achieved."[65] Among the solutions the authors offer is "rebalancing" the data. This can be done by changing the base rates or applying them separately.[66] Another adjustment that could be made is called "in-processing" — that is, building fairness adjustments into the algorithms themselves.[67] They provide the following example:

> [R]isk forecasts for particular individuals that have substantial uncertainty can be altered to improve fairness. If whether or not an individual is projected as high risk depends on little more than a coin flip, the forecast of high risk can be changed to low risk to serve some fairness goal.... One can embed this idea in a classification procedure so that explicit trade-offs are made.... But this too can have unacceptable consequences for false positive and false negative rates.[68]

Another method to increase fairness might be to introduce a "fairness regularizer," which acts as a sort of mathematical penalty when there are "inappropriate associations between membership in a protected group class and the response or legitimate predictors."[69] But the authors acknowledge that this, too, can lead to unequal treatment.[70] Yet another possibility would be the inclusion of "fairness constraints"[71]:

> Fairness, which can be defined in several different ways, translates into a set of linear constraints imposed on accuracy that can also be represented as

---

64 *Ibid.*, p.19.

65 *Ibid.*, p. 23.

66 *Ibid.*, p. 25.

67 *Ibid.*, p. 26.

68 *Ibid.*, p. 26.

69 *Ibid.*, pp. 26–27; see also Kamishima *et al.* (2011).

70 Berk (2013, p. 27).

71 *Ibid.*; Argawal *et al.* (2018).

costs. These fairness-specific costs are weights easily ported to a wide variety of classifiers.[72]

Ultimately, Berk and his colleagues conclude that if we are going to continue to use data infected with historical biases, then it may be that some form of "post-processing" of the results will need to occur.[73] However, even this may not eliminate false positives or negatives.[74]

2019: COMPAS Acknowledges Race Effects

By 2019, there was no longer any real debate that COMPAS and other AI assessment tools produce different results for Black versus white offenders. The explanation was and remains that because Black people have committed more crimes in the past, the models correctly predict higher rates of recidivism for that group in the future. This rationale skillfully omits the fact that the models entrench historical biases and are therefore fundamentally flawed.

The 2019 COMPAS update of its Guide acknowledges the debate and assures its users that they should not be concerned. It adds a new section called "Differential Validity and Fairness Criteria."[75] The Guide instructs that "[t]he risk scale demonstrates predictive fairness if the selection ratio is the same for both groups [Black and white], use fairness if the complements of the positive predictive values are the same in both groups, and model fairness if the false positive and false negative rates are the same for both groups."[76] COMPAS then cites a number of the studies we have discussed, including the one from its own research team.[77] No longer are race discrepancies denied; Northpointe now explains them as relating to "larger base rates."[78] It is odd to use a company's

---

72 Berk (2013, p. 27).

73 *Ibid.*, p. 28.

74 *Ibid.*

75 Guide, p. 17.

76 *Ibid.*, p. 18.

77 *Ibid.*

78 *Ibid.*, p. 1, 18, 20.

own report as if it provides independent support for any proposition, but the Guide does so when it cites Dieterich *et al.*, for the conclusion that:

> [T]his pattern does not show evidence of bias, but rather is the natural consequence of using unbiased scoring rules for groups that happen to have different distribution of scores. These results help explain the effects of the relatively high risk scores and higher base rates of African Americans on the false positive and false negative rates in the Angwin *et al.* (2016) study.[79]

Like the 2015 Guide, the updated version acknowledges that in certain instances, the COMPAS model produces results that are "counter-intuitive" to clinical judgment. It denies that such differences are a result of "the risk score fail[ing] to work properly."[80] It instead explains that, as an actuarial tool, the model is taking general groups of data and applying them to an individual. Factors relating to the offenders age at the time of the current arrest/offense, age at first arrest, history of violence, vocation/education, and history of non-compliance, all contribute to his risk score, but are compared to a data base containing similar information for a much larger population.[81]

The 2019 Guide indicates that each of these inputs is based upon their importance factors as "established by many other researchers in criminal justice."[82] Each factor is assigned a weight:

> The size of the weight is determined by the strength of the item's relationship to person offense recidivism that we observed in our study data. The weighted items are then added together to calculate a risk score.[83]

And a further explanation: "In the context of Violent Recidivism Risk, if you are young, unemployed and have an early-age-at-first-arrest and a history of supervision failure, you could score medium or high on the Violence Risk Scale

---

79 *Ibid.*, p. 19.

80 *Ibid.*, p. 33.

81 *Ibid.*, p. 33, 38.

82 *Ibid.*, p. 33.

83 *Ibid.*

even though you never had a violent offense arrest."[84] Ultimately, the updated Guide is clear about its utilitarian framework and states:

> Risk assessment is about predicting group behavior (identifying groups of higher risk offenders) — it is not about prediction at the individual level. Your risk score is estimated based on known outcomes of groups of offenders who have similar characteristics.[85]

The Guide then looks at whether the tool is "fair" in an unbiased way and whether it can be both "fair" and accurate. The answer, according to COMPAS, quoting the 2018 Berk *et al.*, study is "No: you can't have it all":

> Except in trivial cases, it is impossible to maximize accuracy and fairness at the same time and impossible simultaneously to satisfy all kinds of fairness. In practice, a major complication is different base rates across different legally protected groups.[86]

The Guide states that:

> Risk scales may exhibit race and gender effects because race and gender are correlated with the outcomes that risk scales are designed to predict. Disadvantage in the domains of employment, education, and housing stems from structural inequalities in our society. Constructs within these domains correlate with criminal behavior. In some respects many of the widely accepted criminogenic needs are indirect measures of disadvantage. Risk scale scores use inputs (prior arrest, age at first arrest) and predict outcomes (arrests) that are impacted by intense police practices in some geographical areas. These effects are at the heart of methodological controversies in criminology related to risk assessment and racial bias that have emerged in different contexts over the years.[87]

---

84 *Ibid.*, p. 34.

85 *Ibid.*, p. 35.

86 *Ibid.*, p. 19, quoting Berk (2013, p. 1).

87 *Ibid.*, p. 19 (internal citations omitted).

What this means is simple and disturbing: because Black men supposedly commit crimes at rates that are higher than their representation in the population, there is no way to achieve parity between Black and white defendants. When COMPAS says that "base rates" are different, what it means is that Black people have historically been arrested at higher rates than white people. We know this is an objective truth, but one that reflects embedded biases our country should want to shed; it is not a truth we should seek to entrench.

2020

In February 2020, the Pretrial Justice Institute withdrew its support for use of risk assessment tools:

> Regardless of their science, brand, or age, these tools are derived from data
> reflecting structural racism and institutional inequity that impact our court
> and law enforcement policies and practices. Use of that data deepens that
> inequity.[88]

In March 2020, the MIT Press simultaneously published a pair of articles providing a point and counterpoint on the COMPAS model and fairness: Rudin, Wang, and Coker, "The Age of Secrecy and Unfairness in Recidivism Prediction,"[89] and Jackson, Mendoza, "Setting the Record Straight: What the COMPAS Core Risk and Need Assessment is and is Not."[90] Yet again, the counterpoint is written by Northpointe researchers; Jackson and Mendoza are Northpointe employees.

For Rudin, Wang, and Coker, the "bottom line" of fairness debates is that "there is not a single correct definition of fairness and that multiple types of fairness are incompatible."[91] But, they say, "[w]e put aside typical fairness

---

88 www.pretrial.org/uploads/risk-statement-PJI-2020.

89 www.mitpress.mit.edu/pub/7z10o269/release/3.

90 www.mitpress.mit.edu/pub/hzwo7ax4/release/3.

91 *Ibid.*, p. 3.

considerations for a moment to focus on more pressing issues," including most importantly a lack of transparency in the COMPAS model.[92] Rudin and her colleagues do not view the fairness debate as productive as long as the composition of the model remains unknown.

In an effort to achieve transparency, Rudin and her colleagues perform a partial reconstruction of the COMPAS model. As an initial matter, their primary criticism of the model is that its complexity may result in computational errors. They reference its use of 137 variables and argue that this number of variables alone almost certainly leads to threshold data entry issues, undermining accuracy and trust in the instrument.[93] Specifically, they point to a number of examples in which individuals with lengthy criminal histories are receiving low scores and that this "should be impossible unless inputs have been entered incorrectly or omitted from the COMPAS score altogether."[94] They also point out that some individuals are receiving scores that appear to be unreasonably high given the criminal histories reflected in the database. Finally, Rudin and her colleagues point out that many of the COMPAS questions are proxies for socio-economic success including, for example, "[h]ow hard is it for you to find a job ABOVE minimum wage compared to others?"[95] They conclude that "some form of unfairness caused by COMPAS can affect almost everyone involved in the justice system."[96]

Jackson and Mendoza, in their counterpoint, argue that the COMPAS model is not a black box but a "statistical model with justifiable features" based on "criminological theory."[97] They also refute Rudin *et al.*'s assertions regarding the complexity of the model. They do not refute the inherent unfairness tradeoffs

---

92 *Ibid.*

93 Rudin *et al.* (2020, p. 3). According to Jackson and Mendoza, while the questionnaire may include this number of questions, the instrument is based on 40 (Jackson and Mendoza (2020, p. 9)). They do not, however, explain how they arrive at 40 when the base questionnaire has over 130 response entries.

94 *Ibid.*, p. 24.

95 *Ibid.*, p. 4.

96 *Ibid.*, p. 29.

97 *Ibid.*, p. 8.

that any user of the model must make — that is, trading the ease of mass-scale predictions for the potential of unfairness on an individual level. Nor do they dispute that a database reflecting structural inequalities will necessarily produce results reinforcing those inequalities.

Skeem and Lowenkamp have more recently suggested a series of changes to algorithmic design that might address some of the fairness tradeoffs now openly discussed in the literature.[98] Ultimately, they recommend analyzing the limitations of risk assessment instruments against the alternative they view as also prone to producing racial disparities: human decision-making.[99]

Fairness to the individual requires that the justice system make the best possible individual decision, a decision based on that specific person's history and prospects. Decisions derived from what has happened to a group of people — who we know have been subjected to a host of structural inequalities and biases that are in fact reflected in disproportionate rates of arrest and incarceration — are inconsistent with individual fairness.

In this chapter, I have shown that historical data has now been combined with model design to justify a delta between predictive accuracy and fairness. When tools cannot combine the two — which today they cannot — then use is inappropriate.

It is not enough that their use has become widespread. We have to start over, using essential moral principles to drive tool design. The Declaration of Independence provides that we are all created equal; the U.S. Constitution provides that we are all entitled to equal protection, ensured by due process. The American criminal justice system should view our historical record of bias with shame and seek to start a new. If we accept tools that continue to perpetuate . this history, then we are also accepting a catastrophic denigration of our principles of justice.

---

98 J. Skeem and C. T. Lowenkamp, "Using Algorithms to Address Trade-Offs Inherent in Predicting Recidivism", *Behavioral Sciences & The Law* 38(1) (2020), www.researchgate.net/ publication/309689478_RISK.

99 *Ibid.*

Chapter 11
Lethal Autonomous Weapons and Fairness

⚖

Throughout this book we have discussed AI tools, as they are used in connection with liberty decisions that are designed and used from a utilitarian perspective. I have argued that the core of the American philosophical rights framework is essentially non-utilitarian; instead, it prioritizes justice as fairness — justice at an individual level.

In earlier chapters, we examined the ways in which risk assessment tools fail to protect individual rights. It is my contention that we can and must design AI tools to correspond with our stated core values of individual fairness, particularly when the tools are tasked with making decisions regarding human liberties.

LAWs: The Ultimate AI Utilitarian Tools

Now I want to briefly discuss the ultimate example of AI tools designed according to a utilitarian framework: lethal autonomous weapons (LAWs). LAWs demonstrate the potential for AI to do precisely that which is not being done with risk assessment tools: use advanced technology for the benefit of human liberty, and to bring fairness into areas that are traditionally utilitarian.

LAWs provide an illustrative counterpart to AI used in risk assessment tools. They provide an instance in which, in the military arena where utilitarian doctrine has flourished, AI can cause beneficial movement towards justice as fairness.

Military weaponry has long been designed according to a different set of values than in our criminal justice system. Its purpose is statedly utilitarian: to protect the community — including human life, facilities, and territory — with the least amount of harm inflicted. Deployment of military weaponry is done to protect our whole country's liberty interests, not those of a single person. In this way, the military sphere is fundamentally different from the domestic: the protection of the liberty interests of the individual is subsumed within the protection of those for the community.

We thus have historically accepted that, in order to protect our communities, use of military weapons may — and frequently does — result in collateral damage. In the various recent wars in the Middle East we have seen strikes on residential areas in which military targets are present, but in which unidentified third parties may also be present. We expect that certain strikes will necessarily kill some of each. The reason for this is simple and disheartening: we often lack the ability to kill with the requisite precision. Certain conditions may prevent accurate and clear identification, locations may contain a combination of military and non-military targets, and much weaponry lacks the ability to finely parse intended from unintended targets. A guided missile may limit but not eliminate collateral damage.

The utilitarian design and deployment of LAWs is, then, no surprise. It is the logical continuation of a historical expectation and practice of utilitarian principles in the military arena. However, LAWs present an opportunity for us to reconsider our strictly utilitarian principles in the area of military combat. In the era of AI-enabled military tools, we can and should find ways to reduce collateral damage and bring principles of "justice as fairness" to the military arena.

AI tools, including LAWs, enable military engagement that can increasingly prioritize the protection of individuals.[1] They can do this for several reasons. First, LAWs contain tools that include increased identification accuracy. Second, by taking human decision-making out of the loop, they are able to make careful, dispassionate, and incredibly fast decisions as to whether to engage or not engage a target.[2]

---

1   A very readable and complete book on this topic is: P. Scharre, *Army of None* (New York, New York: Norton Press, 2018).

2   *Ibid.*

The history of warfare has been one of a human-driven weighing of aggregate costs and benefits; the future, however, carries the potential for calculated precision.

Current Use and Potential

LAWs are not the stuff of the near-future; they are already being deployed. Many examples are shrouded by understandable secrecy, but we know of some already in use today: small robotic insects or birds that can fly singly or in swarms and carry light, lethal munitions; drones, missiles, or ships that autonomously locate and engage targets; and small vehicles that can search for, disarm, or deliver bombs.[3] Russia has announced a project to develop autonomous killer robots that can replace human infantry.

Those are just the LAWs that take a physical form, but there are many LAWS that exist in the digital realm alone. Cyber weapons include software that can be inserted into targeted networks or machines, disrupt essential services such as maintaining temperature controls of subterfuges in nuclear programs, interfere with power grids or communications capabilities, or change objectives for other autonomous weapons.[4]

One example of a digital weapon was the "Stuxnet Worm," a digital worm that first came to the awareness of computer security experts in 2010.[5] Stuxnet was designed to take advantage of a particular vulnerability in software that was deployed in connection with control of Iranian nuclear enrichment facilities. The worm itself was capable of spying, stealing, deleting, and changing data. But it could also reach beyond the digital world and into the physical, causing machine malfunctions and significant breakage. The worm worked autonomously — once it was released, it was able to move from one computer to the next, searching for its target. Upon finding its target, it made autonomous decisions about what to steal, change, or disable. The origin of

---

3 *Ibid.*

4 Zetter, *Countdown to Zero Day: Stuxnet and the Launch of the World's First Digital Weapon* (Crown Publishing Group, 2014).

5 *Ibid.*

Stuxnet has never been confirmed, but it is widely believed that the US and Israeli militaries were the creators. Whatever the origin, Stuxnet's designers succeeded in creating a serious setback for the Iranian nuclear enrichment program.

LAWs are useful in warfare precisely because they can enable protective and defensive operations in contested environments in which communications abilities might be compromised. This stands in contrast to our publicly-acknowledged current use of drones to conduct lethal military operations, which require communication capabilities — bandwidth is required for the drone to send back to the operator images of what it is seeing — and a human decision-maker who determines whether to kill a target. That is, a human is always "in the loop" with regard to use and deployment decisions for these weapons. LAWs can now move humans "out of the loop."[6] A drone of perhaps even the same shape and size as its semi-autonomous counterpart no longer needs a human to direct its surveillance operations, identify its target, or make a decision about whether and when to engage.

LAWs have the potential to "do war better" for several reasons. First, their surveillance capabilities are greatly enhanced. AI tools do not get distracted, tired, hungry, or thirsty. They have physical capabilities to surveil with accuracy for lengthy periods of time under inhospitable conditions. AI tools use facial and auditory recognition tools that reduce human guesswork. They are able to process large amounts of information more quickly than a human, and able to act on them faster. Small robotic birds and insects can enter areas that humans cannot, and can bring cameras and other surveillance equipment. They can also engage in camouflaged maneuvers that a human could never achieve.

Second, when actionable information is obtained, AI tools can respond more quickly than a human. Fear and safety concerns are also taken out of decision-making. Third, LAWs allow us to send non-humans into harm's way in

---

6   Johnson, Rapid Assessment Process (RAP) Report #03-10, "Unmanned Effects (UFX): Taking the Human Out of the Loop," (2003); United States Air Force, RPA Vector, Vision and Enabling Concepts 2013–2038 (2014); U.S. Dep't of Defense, "Unmanned Systems Integrated Roadmap, 2017–2042" (2020).

order to protect human interests.[7] True autonomy allows AI to engage in split-second battlefield decisions in ways that supervised weaponry cannot. It seems certain that the combination of these AI-enhanced tools will result in saving human lives. But they also carry with them a serious set of concerns and costs.[8]

A main concern is that the ability to use AI tools to kill is unlikely to remain solely within the military sphere. History teaches us that tools of military origin — guns, supervised drones, and tanks, to name a few — often end up as domestic law-enforcement tools. There is no reason to imagine that LAWs would be different; civilians are likely to find a way to bring them into the domestic sphere. Unleashing LAWs within our communities could have serious consequences. Domestically, however, we have the ability to use regulatory regimes to prohibit access. There is no Second Amendment right to your very own killer robot. Prohibiting domestic use of AI tools that can kill is absolutely necessary to maintaining an ordered society.

LAWS pose serious ethical and justice-based questions within the military sphere as well. How do we ensure that such weapons are deployed only in a manner that is compliant with the laws of war? When the United States used a drone to kill a leading Iranian Major General — Qassim Suleimani — in January 2020 as part of a targeted assassination, he was not on a battlefield, and we were not engaged in a war with Iran. We just thought he was really dangerous, that he was responsible for the deaths of a number of people and that he would be responsible for more if he lived. A lot of people around the world fit this bill too; some of them are on US territory. Supervised drones have changed the way we wage war and distribute responsibility for killing.

---

7   U.S. Dep't of Defense, "Unmanned Systems Integrated Roadmap, 2017–2042" (2020), p. 23.

8   See generally: P. W. Singer, *Battlefields of the Future* (Brookings Institution, 2011); P. W. Singer, "Do Drones Undermine Democracy", *The New York Times* (2012); P. W. Singer, "The Future of Wars Will Be Robotic," *CNN* (2015); P. W. Singer, "Humans Can't Escape Killer Robots, But Humans Can Be Held Accountable for Them," *Vice News* (2016); National Science and Technology Foundation, Exec. Office of the President, "Preparing for the Future of Artificial Intelligence(2016); Human Rights Watch, "Making the Case: The Danger of Killer Robots and the Need for a Preemptive Ban" (2016); International Human Rights Clinic, "Heed the Call: A Moral Imperative to Ban Killer Robots" (2018); B. Docherty, International Human Rights Clinic, "The Need for and Elements of a New Treaty on Fully Autonomous Weapons" (2020).

The Moral Debate

Given the moral and practical issues surrounding weapons that can, without any human involvement, dispense the ultimate deprivation of liberty — death — many believe the only solution is a total ban of LAWs.[9] In 2015, 3,000 AI experts joined together to sound the clarion call:

> If any major military power pushes ahead with AI weapon development, a global arms race is virtually inevitable, and the endpoint of this technological trajectory is obvious: autonomous weapons will become the Kalashnikovs of tomorrow. Unlike nuclear weapons, they require no costly or hard-to-obtain raw materials, so they will become ubiquitous and cheap for all significant military powers to mass-produce.[10]

Chief among the concerns with LAWs are the moral agency and human dignity that many believe machines will never be able to achieve, and without which they will lack the ability to make decisions we consider to be moral. The Human Rights Watch warned: "Fully autonomous weapons, as inanimate machines, could comprehend neither the value of individual life not the significance of its loss."[11] In 2013, in a report to the Human Rights Council, the Special Rapporteur on Extrajudicial Killing stated: "[D]elegating this process [of killing, to machines] dehumanizes armed conflict even further and precludes a moment of deliberation in those cases where it may be feasible. Machines lack morality or mortality, and should as a result, not have life and death powers over humans."[12] Some make the contrary argument: since LAWs lack human feelings, they will therefore be able to carry out missions without the post-traumatic impacts that many humans experience when it comes to killing.

---

9   Human Rights Watch, "Making the Case: The Danger of Killer Robots and the Need for a Preemptive Ban" (2016); International Human Rights Clinic, "Heed the Call: A Moral Imperative to Ban Killer Robots" (2018).

10 Future of Life Institute, "Autonomous Weapons: An Open Letter from AI & Robotics Researchers", July 28, 2015, http://futureoflife.org/open-letter-autonomous-weapons (last accessed August 2020).

11 Human Rights Watch, "Making the Case: The Dangers of Killer Robots and the Need for a Preemptive Ban" (2016), www.hrw.org/report/2016/12/09/making-case/dangers-killer-robots-and-need-preemptive-ban), p. 20.

12 C. Heynds, "Report of the Special Rapporteur on Extrajudicial Summary or Arbitrary Executions", Human Rights Council, 23rd Session, United Nations, General Assembly (2013), www.ohcr.org/session23/A-HRC-23-47_en.

There are many practical concerns about the use of truly autonomous weapons as well. They center around the following general issues:

1. **Distinguishing a target:** How will LAWs be able to distinguish human targets that may be engaging in specific human behaviors such as hiding, surrendering, or deciding to disengage and retreat? That is, how will we teach the AI to distinguish a target that they should engage with, from one that either they should not or should no longer?

2. **Understanding the context:** How will LAWs be able to understand if the moment for deployment has changed in subtle ways, no longer requiring the need for a lethal response? How can we teach the AI about the value of one target versus another and how the value of a target can shift during the course of an event?

3. **Proportionality:** How can AI be taught to balance competing values such as a successful strike against the possibility of collateral damage in the form of human deaths? How do we teach AI to balance civilian harm with military advantage?

4. **Accountability:** If human decision-makers are taken out of the process, who is responsible for any death or destruction that results? The concept of accountability incorporates legal responsibility along with moral and ethical responsibility. Holding the AI itself accountable is clearly an inadequate answer — it cannot be hailed into a court or international tribunal to account for its actions. A lethal autonomous weapon that commits a murder cannot be jailed — there is no retributive justice apart from trying to "turn it off" that can be meted out against the weapon itself. Since a truly autonomous weapon would be engaging in its own decision-making, its human designers would not be truly accountable for a specific act. (Perhaps they would bear moral accountability for the initial deployment and release into the world — but that is something quite different.)

5. **System Failure:** How will humans respond to the inevitable failure of a deployed system? Can it be hacked into and its decision-making processes altered in some way?[13]

---

13 Human Rights Watch, "Making the Case: The Dangers of Killer Robots and the Need for a Preemptive Ban" (2016), www.hrw.org/report/2016/12/09/making-case/dangers-killer-robots-and-need-preemptive-ban), pp. 6–23.

Each of these concerns is valid and needs to be answered. But the fact is, these weapons have and will become available in various parts of the world. Once one country has them, all will view them as necessary. Every country with the necessary resources will try and obtain them. No country will want to be without tools that may provide decided advantages to an adversary.

Since we cannot turn back the clock from the LAWs that exist or that are under development, we are best served by moving the dialogue to how we can shape them to best conform with our value system. Right now, we have the ability to use LAWs to make war more precise, avoiding unnecessary collateral damage and bringing increased fairness to individual targets and those in their vicinity. We must act to do so.

The Legal Framework

Intertwined with the moral debate about the development and use of LAWs are legal questions. Specifically, what legal status do they have, and what rules apply to their use?

Domestic use is governed by all of the state and federal laws relating to privacy (surveillance), weaponry (gun laws), and laws relating to explosive devices. There is no doubt that the existing legal framework in the United States would prevent personal use of one's very own killer robot. That same framework would also prevent invasions of personal privacy that could come with robotic insects that enter one's home. It is nonetheless concerning to imagine a world in which LAWs are available on the black market or can be made out of relatively accessible parts and technology. There will be a race to stay one step ahead of those who will seek to violate prohibitions on use, ownership, and access.

Military use also must comply with legal frameworks governing the conduct of war. The law of war and conflict is an enormously complicated area. For purposes of this discussion, I will focus on only a few points. First, while in recent years the United States has opted out of, failed to sign, or withdrawn from a number of international treaties, it remains bound to certain key components of international law. The Martens Clause of the Geneva

Convention is widely considered the most applicable provision of international law that prohibits use of lethal autonomous weapons in a manner that will violate core humanitarian principles. This clause is designed to provide a "failsafe" mechanism — covering unanticipated situations — and provides that:

> In cases not covered by this Protocol or other international agreements, civilians and combatants remain under the protection and authority of the principles of international law derived from established custom, from the principles of humanity and from the dictates of public conscience.[14]

The Third Geneva Convention encompasses associated statutes that establish the International Committee of the Red Cross ("ICRC"), a Swiss non-governmental organization, as both a protector of people during times of war and an essential guardian and monitor of international humanitarian law. A core humanitarian principle of the ICRC is to treat populations humanely — that is, with compassion and respect. Lethal autonomous weapons, however used, must comply with this core principle.

International human rights law also provides for a right to life (codified in Article 6 of the International Covenant on Civil and Political Rights ("ICCPR")). The ICCPR states that "Every human being has the inherent right to life," and "No one shall be arbitrarily deprived of his life."[15] In times of war, security forces may deprive someone of life only if to do so is necessary to protect human life, it constitutes a last resort, and is proportionate to the threat. Arbitrary killings are a violation of international human rights law. Both the Universal Declaration of Human Rights ("UDHR") and the ICCPR require that states "ensure that any person whose rights or freedoms... are violated shall have an effective remedy."[16] The right to a remedy includes some method of holding an actor who has committed a wrong accountable. The UDHR provides for a principle of personal dignity.

---

14 See M. N. Schmitt & J. S. Thurnher, "Out of the Loop: Autonomous Weapons Systems and the Law of Armed Conflict", *Harvard Nat'l Sec. Journal*, 4 (2013), 243–250.

15 ICCPR, Article 6 (adopted, 2018).

16 ICCPR, Article 2(3).

LAWs therefore must be designed and used in ways that conform with these internationally-recognized humanitarian principles. As discussed below, designs can include instructions regarding acceptable parameters for engagement or disengagement. Humans have learned acceptable laws of war; we can similarly teach those lessons to machines.

Towards Acceptable Design and Use

Lethal autonomous weapons thus present a series of moral and legal challenges that are far from resolved. As the human progenitors of such tools, we have the ability to design them in a manner best suited to allowing them to optimize fairness. As we discussed in earlier chapters, AI learns what humans teach it.

First, we can teach AI weaponry rules that guide moral decision-making and decision-making that prioritizes fairness to individuals. One way to do this is to move away from consequentialist decision-making associated with utilitarian frameworks, and to prioritize the means by which the objective is achieved. When the means to the end are taken into consideration, LAWs inevitably move towards individual fairness. So, for instance, LAWs can be trained not to blow up an entire area in order to kill a single target, but to seek a more precise way to engage the target. We can teach AI that the means it uses matter.

A major way to achieve individual fairness is to take into consideration the particular circumstances of the target (whether it be person, territory, or facility). Below I set forth four principles that can be used as non-exclusive guides in this regard[17]:

1. **Lethal force may only be used if there is no other way to achieve an objective:** This principle recognizes that AI tools that are capable of autonomous use of lethal force ought to be capable of autonomous use of non-lethal force as well. There should always be an assessment of whether

---

17 Ronald Arkin speaks and writes extensively on use and design of lethal autonomous weapons. He, too, has suggested design parameters that would include ethical frameworks and moral bounding. (R. Arkin, "People Behaving Badly, Robots Behaving Better?" (July 12, 2013), www.youtube.com/watch?time continue=4&v=zrD62oXUZkQ&feature=emb logo); "The Interaction Hour: Don't Call Them Killer Robots," www.youtube.com/watch?v=ax -uPzWmyw).

non-lethal force may achieve an objective, and if so, then to use it. AI should not be used to kill when it can force surrender instead. This principle would allow a targeted individual to have an opportunity to disengage or submit, which can thereby result in a saved life.

2. **Lethal force must be used in the way that is most likely to avoid collateral damage:** This principle recognizes that the type of precision of which AI weaponry may be capable in certain situations should be utilized whenever possible. It also recognizes that the lives of individuals unrelated to the achievement of an objective should be given value.

3. **Lethal force may not be used with regard to any human object that is prone or is under four feet tall and does not have an identifiable weapon or explosive device:** This principle recognizes that a person who is potentially injured and therefore unable to engage in lethal attack should not be killed. It also recognizes that killing of children should be avoided in all but the most extreme and extraordinary circumstances. This principle further prioritizes particular characteristics and circumstances of a target and seeks ways to avoid lethal engagement.

4. **Lethal force may not be used in a manner that is anticipated to cause unreasonable pain and suffering:** This principle recognizes that certain circumstances may make the use of lethal force unreasonably painful in light of an objective. The term "unreasonable" suggests that the AI tool would weigh the importance of the objective against the likelihood of pain and suffering. This calculation would be done with regard to the individual circumstances of the target.

Prioritizing the means over the ends requires LAWs to run what is in effect a moral calculation with regard to specific targets. In doing so, it has the ability to move the framework we consider for deployment of military weaponry further away from utilitarian and in the direction of individual fairness. We cannot stop war, but we can use AI tools to make it fair.

Chapter 12
Conclusion

⚖⚖

In previous chapters, we have seen that AI tools are actively being used to make decisions that impact the most sacred personal rights any human has: life and liberty. Decisions impacting life and liberty must be based on ethical and justice-based frameworks of fairness and protection of an individual's constitutional rights.

We have seen that AI assessment tools have been designed against a utilitarian framework of justice: they sacrifice concepts of fairness to the individual for an overall concept of reduced crime within a community. These tools have been designed and deployed without any national agreement on standards, and there is no current mechanism that provides legal accountability for the unfairness that may result. The call to action for risk and needs assessment tools is to set standards designed for fairness. The demand is that we do not accept arguments that tools are already in use; that it's too hard to go back now; that the predictive accuracy is good enough. We can and must do more than this.

In contrast to risk and needs assessment tools, a significant amount of attention is being paid to the appropriate design standards and deployment framework for AI tools that can be used to kill us: lethal autonomous weapons. Whether we like it or not, these weapons are being developed by private contractors and state-financed researchers and military personnel all over the world.

In contrast to risk assessment tools, the debate surrounding LAWs is steeped in well-established rules of war, engagement and international humanitarian law.

As a new type of weaponry that can increase accuracy and speed of decision-making, LAWs present an opportunity to move away from the established utilitarian military framework and towards individualized fairness. The call to action for LAWs is to change the debate from whether to ban the weaponry outright, and instead focus on how to maximize these tools' capacities for fairness in ultimate decisions about life and death.

We are AIs birth parents. We can design it to be fair, and we can design it to be just.

Suggested Additional Reading

⚖️

A. Agrawal, J. Gans, and A. Goldfarb, *Prediction Machines: The Simple Economics of Artificial Intelligence* (Boston, MA: HBR Press, 2018).

J. Bentham, *The Principles and Morals of Legislation* (Amherst, NY: Prometheus Books, 1988).

C. M. Bishop, *Pattern Recognition and Machine Learning* (New York, NY: Springer, 2006).

D. J. Chalmers, *The Conscious Mind: In Search of a Fundamental Theory* (Oxford: Oxford University Press, 1997).

A. Damasio, *Self Comes to Mind: Constructing the Conscious Brain* (New York, NY: Vintage Books, 2010).

P. Domingos, *The Master Algorithm: How the Quest for the Ultimate Learning Machine Will Remake our World* (New York, NY: Basic Books, 2018).

R. Dworkin, *Justice for Hedgehogs* (Cambridge, MA: Harvard University Press, 2013).

S. Gerrish, *How Smart Machines Think* (Cambridge, MA: MIT Press, 2018).

H. L. A. Hart, *Essays in Jurisprudence and Philosophy* (Oxford: Oxford University Press, 2001).

H. L. A. Hart and J. Gardner, *Punishment and Responsibility: Essays in the Philosophy of Law*, 2nd edn. (Oxford: Oxford University Press, 2009).

J. Heaton, *Artificial Intelligence for Humans, Volume 3: Deep Learning and Neural Networks* (St. Louis, MO: Heaton Research, 2015).

J. LeDoux, *The Deep History of Ourselves: The Four-Billion-Year Story of How We Got Conscious Brains* (New York, NY: Viking, 2019).

G. D. Marino (ed.), *Ethics: The Essential Writings* (New York, NY: Modern Library, 2010).

M. Mitchell, *Artificial Intelligence: A Guide for Thinking Humans* (New York, NY: Farrar, Straus and Giroux, 2019).

J. Rawls, *A Theory of Justice*, Rev. edn. (Cambridge, MA: Harvard University Press, 1971).

S. J. Russell and P. Norvig, *Artificial Intelligence: A Modern Approach*, 3rd edn. (India: Person Education, 2018).

P. Scharre, *Army of None: Autonomous Weapons and the Future of War* (New York, NY: W.W. Norton & Company, 2019).

S. Schneider, *Artificial You: AI and the Future of Your Mind* (Princeton, NJ: Princeton University Press, 2019).

J. R. Searle, *The Construction of Social Reality* (New York, NY: The Free Press, 1995).

J. R. Searle, *The Mystery of Consciousness* (New York, NY: NYREV, 1997).

J. R. Searle, *Mind: A Brief Introduction* (Oxford: Oxford University Press, 2004).

T. J. Sejnowski, *The Deep Learning Revolution* (Cambridge, MA: MIT Press, 2018).

P. Singer, *Ethics in the Real World: 82 Brief Essays on Things That Matter* (Princeton, NJ: Princeton University Press, 2016).

M. Tegmark, *Life 3.0: Being Human in the Age of Artificial Intelligence* (New York, NY: Alfred A. Knopf, 2017).

Printed in the United States
by Baker & Taylor Publisher Services